FINDING
the pieces

KIMBERLY S WHITAKER

Finding the Pieces

Trilogy Christian Publishers A Wholly Owned Subsidiary of Trinity Broadcasting Network

2442 Michelle Drive Tustin, CA 92780

Rights Department, 2442 Michelle Drive, Tustin, CA 92780.

Trilogy Christian Publishing/TBN and colophon are trademarks of Trinity Broadcasting Network.

Design by: Kelly Stewart

Photo by: Greg Travis

For information about special discounts for bulk purchases, please contact Trilogy Christian Publishing.

10 9 8 7 6 5 4 3 2 1

Library of Congress Cataloging-in-Publication Data is available.

ISBN: 979-8-88738-892-2

E-ISBN: 979-8-88738-893-9

DEDICATION

The dedication should be easy.
Every rule says it should be short and to the point.

There are *special ones* to be found in the acknowledgments,
but this book is dedicated to you.

Each one of you holding this book has been the encourager
who placed the pen within my hand.

How could I select just one name?
I could list a thousand and still not be done.

This book is dedicated to each of you; all treasured pieces of my life...
some living and some gone.

Thank you for helping me find my pieces.

ACKNOWLEDGMENTS

When people ask what Finding the Pieces is about, my answer has often been a challenge. It is NOT a typical memoir, nor did I sit down with a plan and start writing it. This book evolved from a lifetime of stories and posts and the urging from others to compile them.

So, the first *Grazie* must be to the folks in my life who encouraged me to take on the task of writing my first book! Here she is!

My second thank you would be to all the *real-life characters* contained within the pages of this book. Without you, I would have no story. Without you, many of *my pieces* would be missing. Thank you. I love you each so very much.

To **Shelbi Chandlee, Jennifer Hudson, Rachel Hiatt and the team at TBN/Trilogy**; thank you for your time, patience and guidance and for *teaching me how to write a book!* I know I have been quite a challenge. *Grazie!*

Thank you, **Greg Travis**, for helping me put the final pieces together on the cover and for your expertise in photo sizing! So thankful you were *placed in my path.*

Don Finto, Micheal W. and Debbie Smith. What joy you have added to my life. You are such great examples of faith and leadership to the world. So thankful to have you in a little corner of mine.

Nelson and Mariana Eddy. Your advice, encouragement and expertise has been such a blessing all along the way.

I love you guys. You set the standard of what a marriage should look like, from the very first handshake. Yes, Nelson, I remember that! *That's all folks!*

Steve and Gena Vineyard. You may have provided *steel* for the masses, but you assisted me in the opportunity of building a new *life. Thank you.*

Alexander. Thank you for seeing and reminding me of who I truly am and for showing me the castles.

Jean Ann...thanks for the immediate comment. *You are such a Barnabas.*

T&A. Thanks for the tangents and for your faith in me.

Riccardo, Paola and Francesco. How did I ever become so blessed as to have found you? You are truly *mi famiglia.* **Dani, Gianna and *Carlatina* too.** Muah!

My precious **Hallie and Addie Grace and baby boy.** You inspire me! While it's hard for *Nonna* to be so far away from you, I pray for the day when I can share Italy with you and open new doors of adventure! Dream BIG little ones!

My immediate family. **Mom, Dad and Kathryne.** Thank you for putting up with that crazy, wide-open and wide-eyed dreamer from day one. You have loved, supported and encouraged me through every peak and valley. Most importantly, you have each instilled the love of the Father into me and have been beautiful examples of faith through adversity. How blessed I am to have been born into this family.

My **Joseph and Clay.** That the Father loved me so much as to entrust me as your mother will always be one of the greatest gifts in my life. *You are some of my most cherished* *pieces.* I pray you will always find comfort under my wing, love in my heart and kindness in my words. May my journey encourage you along yours and always lead you to Abba who makes *all things new.*

And last, but definitely NOT least. For **God the Father, the Son, and the Holy Spirit**...who allowed me into darkness to see them more clearly. Thank you for the precious gift of brokenness which changed my life forever. In it, and because of your infinite mercy and grace, I can see the entire image. *Thanks be to God.*

ENDORSEMENTS

BLESSING OVER THE READER

You are about to embark on a journey with our dear and gifted friend, Kim Whitaker. Her story is laid out on the following pages, and although she will take you overseas and in and out of heartache, the truth is Kim's history is *HISstory*...God shows up in every chapter because Kim is His beloved child. He has been fitting the pieces of Kim's life together and is continuing to guide her steps, whether in Italy or Nashville. (Location doesn't matter when the heart belongs to Jesus!)

So, may God open your eyes and heart to the beauty of the story of one life committed to walking every day in step with Him and bless you with the grace to do the same. Enjoy the journey!

—MICHAEL W. AND DEBBIE SMITH

BLESSING OVER THE WORDS

I don't know that I've ever met anyone who makes a more joyful impression than Kim Whitaker. She spreads joy everywhere she goes—when she has friends over to enjoy her masterpiece creations, when she is describing a recent journey to Italy or some gathering with friends from wherever, but especially when she is talking about her Lord. When I first met Kim, I would never have imagined some of the disappointments and challenges and grief that had been a part of her life. She had and has so surrendered those hard places to God and has seen Him weave them into a tapestry of joy that she now spreads with every breath. Come along for the voyage with this woman of faith, this woman of joy, this woman of destiny. And you may end up being a bit changed yourself.

May this story and these words glorify the Father and enrich the lives of everyone who reads them.

God bless you, Kim!

—DON FINTO

TABLE OF CONTENTS

NOT A FOREWORD—A FORWARD

As a writer, I believe a powerful and compelling story requires everything we have. It demands the best of us. I don't know, but I may have even said that at some point to Kim when I was her senior high school English teacher.

Until Kim shared her story and the manuscript for this book with me, I didn't realize just how true that observation about writing was. Truly, the life journey that has become this book didn't just require Kim's best—*it took it.* It demanded her fairytale marriage be destroyed in nightmarish fashion, her self-confidence be swallowed up in self-doubt, her beautiful family be torn apart, successful business abandoned, dreams given way to despair, and joy to anguish. The life she believed in and thought she knew was twisted into something unrecognizable.

But this is a story of redemption and not defeat. So, what changed the course of Kim's journey? Travel. Taking wing to Italy began the process of *Finding the Pieces* for Kim.

This is a travel book. But not in the conventional sense. Yes, in the pages that follow, you'll be treated to the beauty and wonder of Tuscany's rolling hills and the joy and depth of the Italian people—you'll experience both in adventurous stories and poignant photos. But those travels, while intimate and enriching, are secondary to the bigger journey and the real story here.

The real story is *how* Kim has navigated life since her breaking. Simply put, she doesn't navigate. She invited God to steer by means of a very simple daily prayer. It's a prayer that's transported and transformed her and moved many others. This prayer has moved her closer to the Father and more in touch with herself simply by moving *outside of herself.*

Her prayer is simply this—*that each day God would place someone in her path that either needs her in their life or whom she needs in hers.* Read on, and you'll discover all of the wonderful places and people that specific prayer and total dependence on the Father has taken her.

Who knows, this prayer and book might transport you as well. I know it has moved, changed, and challenged me. The talented and hopeful high school senior who was once my student is now the talented and hopeful woman, tempered by truth and guided by prayer, *who has now become my teacher.*

Ready to go? Let's. And travel mercies as we do.

NELSON EDDY
1982 DAVID LIPSCOMB HIGH SCHOOL ENGLISH TEACHER,
NASHVILLE, TENNESSEE
WRITER, MANAGING PARTNER-CREATIVE
AT DVL SEIGENTHALER—FINN PARTNERS (1986—)

RESPONSE TO THE FORWARD

My dearest teacher,

Because you have experienced this place, you can imagine me sitting at the kitchen table here in Tavarnelle. I am facing the setting sun in the late heat of the day.

I just finished a *tiny* bit of editing the foreword; *calming down*, as you put it.

Although your original words are my exact feelings and truths, they may be too difficult for some to read, so they have been gently edited.

I am in a complete puddle. Not just because of your beautiful words but because God *steered the boat* in the direction of your writing them. The very use of the word "navigation" in *your* writing was occurring as they were written!

I was clearly disappointed when Michael told me he would be unable to write the foreword due to preparation for his world tour after the two-year pandemic. Of course, he graciously offered to help in any way possible, and did.

Just as in a million other *plan Bs* in my life, God was in complete control. To be honest, even though Michael W. Smith is one of the most gifted writers living today, I don't believe *he was meant to write those words*. Although a cherished new friend, Michael did not know me or my story nearly as intimately as you do.

I believe God put the pen in *your* hand. *The foreword for this book was meant to come from you...* the teacher who instilled the very love of writing in my heart over forty years ago.

Thank you, dear teacher. This is everything. Although I am unworthy of *your* words, I do hope that *mine* will be an encouragement for others to survive...and not only survive but flourish!

Your always and ever devoted student and friend,

Kim

MY SWEET MAMA WORKING A PUZZLE.

INTRODUCTION

My mother loves working on jigsaw puzzles, and last Christmas, I had one waiting on her when she arrived for a visit. She left before completing it, and one evening, even with my super-busy Christmas schedule, I sat down to finish it. I needed to decompress. There was only a tiny portion left to complete. *I thought* it would only take a minute; I would finish it, take it apart, then put it away.

As I began working, I discovered that a few edge pieces she placed, which *did fit exactly side-by-side, did not fit* once I tried fitting in the final ones underneath.

This crafty puzzle maker intentionally made several ways to trick the *enigmatologist* (puzzle solver). Although they *appeared to* fit one way, it was only when trying to place the *inside* pieces, the mistakes were revealed, causing the need to *take it apart* and completely restructure the border. *What a light bulb moment this was for me!*

As I crawled into bed that night, I thanked God for this important revelation. I literally imagined Him taking Mother's hand in His and placing those pieces so I could finally see the big picture. God used a Christmas puzzle to illustrate this life-changing truth to me.

The outside pieces of my puzzle are mostly now in place, and I am *finally* beginning to see the inside pieces come together. I am still not certain what the image is, but that really doesn't matter. I'm fine with waiting.

I know without a shadow of a doubt my life will be a glorious masterpiece because I know The Artist *personally*.

The stories written within these pages are those pieces. Just as in a jigsaw puzzle, each person, every story and memory, is a vital piece *dependent* on the other.

The reality is, *my* story was written before I was born.

The people and characters God has placed in my path from the time of my birth are very specific to my journey. He provided and allowed every piece, *both good and bad*.

I now understand some that *I thought* were the *final outside pieces*; many that I might have forced into place had to be *rearranged*. I also realize many of these pieces *did fit...if only for a season*.

I gratefully acknowledge and understand *every piece has served a purpose* and has ultimately worked together to make the *entire image created by The Master complete*.

I am thankful for *all* the pieces, which is such a *huge* breakthrough.

I pray these pieces of my journey will encourage you on yours.

ALL ROADS LEAD TO ROME

CHAPTER 1

All Roads Lead to Rome

Promise me that you'll always remember: you're braver than you believe, stronger than you seem, and smarter than you think.

—WINNIE-THE-POOH

On August 24, 2015, I loaded the final box and my English cocker, Weazy, into my Honda Pilot and headed north. A twenty-five-foot truck containing all my worldly possessions and the Muscled-Up Movers crew followed behind, headed to Nashville, Tennessee.

Like most August days in Alabama, the air was thick and steamy, which felt like one last sucker punch in the gut. Honestly, I was glad to be leaving.

As I entered the I-65 ramp, I turned on the radio to pass the time while driving. My radio is usually set on a classical, jazz, or Christian station, but this time, for some reason, it landed on XM's *The Highway*. Loud and clear was Rascal Flatts asking God to bless the road that led directly to Him!

For years I have felt God speak to me through music

and lyrics, and I was certain that this country song on my car radio that day was a nod that I was headed in the right direction. Even though I wasn't returning to a lost love, my *broken road was leading me back home.*

Born and raised in Music City, it felt right to call Nashville home after nearly thirty years away from her. An added bonus was that both of my sons, my parents, immediate family, and many close friends were waiting there for me, which lent an extra measure of comfort, especially when starting life over again at fifty-two.

Although the reason for my return home was *not a part of my plan*, I tried my best not to let fears and doubts get the better of me. I actually drew encouragement from the idea of new adventures and was excited about the move.

JUMPING OFF

It must be noted that I have never been one to shy away from a new challenge or adventure.

My mother still laughs while recounting this childhood story which illustrates this so well.

I was approximately four years old when invited to my first birthday slumber party. Being a *bag lady* from birth, I am certain my suitcase was packed on Monday and contained everything but the kitchen sink!

The event was not only a sleepover but also a swimming party. The morning after the sleepover, we headed to the Johnson Pool, a private swimming club in the East Tennessee town of Athens. I still vividly recall the mixed smell of chlorine and spring foliage in bloom around the pool. This is a sensory memory that is still so strong to this day.

When my mom arrived for pick up, I was in a mid-air swan dive off the high-diving board! The birthday girl's mother commented, "Kim is such an excellent swimmer! Where did she take lessons?" Stunned and nauseated, my mother replied, "Um, Kim has *never* taken any lessons and does *not* know how to swim!" A huge splash only added to Mom's shock!

As I *Esther Williamsed* my way over to the edge of the pool and wiggled out, I knew my sweet mother was given an early premonition of things to come with her baby girl, *Fearless Fiona!* The odd thing is, I am witnessing this exact trait already in my two-year-old red-headed granddaughter. Fear is not a part of her vocabulary, either!

Little did this fearless brown-eyed girl know just how much strength and courage she would be called upon to muster later in life. The truth is, most of life's greatest lessons are learned at a very young age, and many of them will only come to fruition while one is standing on the precipice of a life-changing event.

One of my favorite historical heroines is Florence Nightingale, *the lady with the lamp*. I still have my illustrated book report from the fifth grade, yet another piece of memorabilia, or as my sister calls it *preserved artifacts from my life*.

Florence penned a most profound quote, which made an early impression on me: "How very little can be done when living under the spirit of fear." Such truth.

ENTREPRENEURIAL SPIRIT

Fortunately, I was raised by two hard-working parents who never operated under a *spirit of fear*. Instead, they operated under an entrepreneurial spirit, which in itself is void of fear. Although both attended college, they were self-taught in many different areas. Dad was a city boy and the middle of five children. I am certain he learned early to take care of himself and fix things. Perhaps Mom, growing up a farm girl during the depression, instilled invaluable lessons of hard work and dedication.

I can still picture a homemade paper towel holder she created from a wire coat hanger nailed to a pine tree when we were camping. Funny are the memories that make lasting impressions on the heart of a child.

With hardly two nickels, my *pioneer parents* also turned a dream into reality by restoring an old two-story clapboard house into an exclusive waiting-list-only kindergarten in an East Tennessee college town. Mom took *homeschooling*, which was not even a thing yet, to a new level. She not only taught the ABCs but also taught art, music, reading, and manners, *and* prepared hot lunches for over thirty hungry little ones every day, including me! Even with her busy schedule, my mother never shirked her responsibilities at home.

In 1974, Dad made a huge leap of faith by leaving his job with TVA when they wanted to relocate him to Alaska and moved us to Nashville. He knew this would offer my sister and me more educational and cultural opportunities. I realize their decisions and leaps of faith have played a giant role in who I am today. I think he also knew the Eskimo climate would never work for his three girls!

Their *can-do and adventurous spirit* was definitely instilled in me.

Over the last forty years, I have owned and operated several small businesses, ultimately leading to the creation of Haul Couture in 2009, a successful national bag brand. Although its life was cut short much earlier than I had anticipated *or wanted*, I do know that in it were so many lessons learned, people met, and purposes fulfilled. I also believe it was preparing me for the *rest of my life*.

One of the greatest lessons learned with Haul Couture was *action*. I took an idea and *acted* on it. I didn't just sit around and dream about it. I actively pursued it, did the work, and with the help of an amazing team, turned it into a reality. Although challenging, those years were some of the most rewarding of my life.

ALL ROADS LEAD TO ROME

World-famous speaker and lecturer Dale Carnegie said, "Inaction breeds doubt and fear. Action breeds confidence and courage. If you want to conquer fear, do not sit at home and think about it. Go out and get busy."

On August 23, 2019, almost four years to the date I had arrived to Nashville, I headed down yet another very unexpected road.

This time, the road led *south* on the A1 Autostrada, which connects Florence, Italy (*not Alabama*), to Rome! I vividly remember a giant knot in my stomach as I inched closer to Rome, thinking to myself, *I am driving into Rome by myself! What in the world am I thinking?*

All of a sudden, an overwhelming peace came over me. I literally heard a voice say, "Kim, this is just like any other road you have ever driven. It is *no* different. Just breathe and trust me. You've got this! I've got *you*!"

While driving, I remembered wheeling into New York City as a senior in high school with three best friends and Mom, Dot Dot Kay. I also recalled maneuvering a twenty-five-foot moving truck during rush-hour traffic in Houston, Texas, during a tropical storm!

I giggled as I pictured myself backing a twenty-foot trailer hitched to the back of my Honda Pilot off of Peachtree Boulevard down into a tiny space at the International Gift Market in Atlanta. I am certain I was singing *Jesus, Take the Wheel!*

I recentered, tightly gripped the steering wheel of that tiny rental car, and drove right into the heart of Rome! I did not miss one turn and landed exactly where I planned to go, which was only two blocks away from the Spanish Steps.

I'll admit, I was super anxious to connect with my travel companion and gulp down a big glass of Chianti and let out a huge sigh of relief...but I had done it. I made it all by myself! Well, not really. *Not ever all by myself.*

The biggest accomplishment of my safe arrival into Rome that day was *not* arriving at the destination. *Anyone* can follow Google Maps or Waze.

My greatest accomplishment was not giving in to the doubt and fear that would keep me from making the trip in the first place!

Doubt and fear are so stealthy and cunning! They creep into the crevices of our minds and paralyze us when our feet are on unsettled ground.

These doubts and fears completely rob us of our joy. They are common to almost all of us at one time or another. However, they serve absolutely no purpose.

Overcoming these obstacles has led me into the new life in which I am now living.

When I post about my time in Italy on Facebook and someone comments, "You're so lucky!" It sends me into a tizzy!

There is no *luck* in what I have experienced. There has been blood, sweat, and many tears. I am living this life because I did not roll over and die...and I could have. Be assured, there were *many* days when that was exactly what I wanted to do.

People ask, "What is your book about?"

I do find that a difficult question to answer and often stutter around trying to explain the genre of my book and the *whys* of my writing it.

I guess the first reason which comes to mind is *I am a born storyteller.*

I have always communicated best through the written word and my art; they go hand in hand. My photography is another form of art and communication, and Lord only knows I have volumes of that to share.

I have been encouraged by friends for years to compile and publish some of my thoughts and stories, many of which seem impossible to believe, even to me.

When my boys were young, one of their best buddies, who spent a lot of time at our house, said, *"Mrs. Kim, Can I please ride with you today? I love story time in your car!"* Dexter Rowe was such a boost to that tired young mother's fragile ego.

Perhaps the most practical reason for my writing may be that when I was walking through *my storm*, well-meaning friends and family offered self-help and spiritual book after book, trying to provide bits of peace and direction through the chaos that had ripped my life apart. To be honest, although their motives were kind and appreciated, most books were too long and arduous for me to handle. I could barely get through a Psalm or two, which I forced myself to read daily. My ADD was in full force, with thoughts swirling around like a cyclone making my attention span bare minimum on the best day.

I was *living in the Land of Lamentations* and needed short, joy-filled, inspirational stories to lift my spirits and give me *hope* that this mess would not be the *first and last* thing I would think about every day for the rest of my life.

Honestly, I did not set out to write this book. My book found me.

PRAYER AND SURRENDER

In the darkest eye of *my storm*, I began to pray a very specific prayer.

I prayed every day that God would place someone in my path (and in the paths of my children) who could help me, *or* someone who might benefit from *my* help.

Every day, this was my prayer.

Every day, He answered it.

Every day.

God's faithfulness to this prayer has been overwhelming and, many times, shocking. As a believer, I shouldn't be surprised, but I *always* am. God's provision still takes my breath away.

For the past eight years, God has assembled a stunning cast of characters, people, and places that could not have been dreamed of or produced by *anyone* other than The Almighty. *Period.*

It was in these answered prayers I truly believe this book was born. Just like the people He scattered along my path, I believe He also provided this opportunity of writing and placed the pen within my hand.

Hope (noun)

1. To believe that what is desired can be had or will turn out for the best

2. A feeling of trust

I guess if I was pressed to give only one reason for spending the last three years hunched over a computer, trying to articulate something that matters...that one reason would be *to give hope.*

Many holding this book are currently riding huge waves of despair and grief that seem impossible to overcome. Some may have received the diagnosis you never dreamed of hearing. Some may be carrying a baby who will never run and play as you had planned. Some, facing financial ruin or mental instability.

Many are sitting at a table that now has an empty chair due to sudden death or divorce...which, at times, to me, seems like one and the same.

There are those dealing with debilitating addiction: their own or of someone they love.

Some of you are living frozen in fear from the effects of the pandemic or political climate, which continues to cast an unending message of doom and gloom.

It may be that life for you is really good right now, but for some reason, you just have the blues and need a little encouragement. Or, perhaps, you wish to encourage someone else along *their* journey.

Several years ago, a wise-beyond-his-years young man who was dealing with trauma of his own made a statement that offered me a very inspiring perspective.

When I asked if he was okay, he replied, "No, but I will be. I think I understand why this has happened."

"Please tell me so I can understand," I replied. He said, "Maybe God allows these things to happen as a reminder that we are really not made for this world."

This belief could not be sustained without the promise found in Joshua 1:9. It was taught to me and has been written on my heart since I was a child. My belief in this promise is the reason I survived *the storm* and have conquered fear and depression.

"Be strong and courageous. Do not be afraid; do not be discouraged, for the LORD your God will be with you wherever you go" (Joshua 1:9, NIV).

So, my friend, when you find yourself driving into the heart of Rome, or drowning in the *eye of your storm*, take heart. *You are not alone.* You have a *Father* who goes before you and is offering you hope, but *only* if you choose to claim it.

Once upon a time, Winnie-the-Pooh wisely said, "You're braver than you believe, stronger than you seem, and smarter than you think."

ONE OF MY DETAILED EARLY DRAWINGS AROUND AGE 4 OR 5.
(NOTICE MOM'S PEARLS!)

CHAPTER 2

It's *All* in the Details

It's the little details that are vital. Little things make big things happen.

—JOHN WOODEN

I have always been a lover of photography. As a young girl, I could often be found with my Kodak Instamatic camera, snapping hundreds of photos in our backyard. God only knows how many rolls of film my poor mother developed, only to find puzzling images of our beautiful... West Meade garbage cans? What *others* failed to see in my shot was the tiny speck of a chipmunk eating an acorn in *front* of the can.

I have *always* seen the tiny details. Well, *most* of them.

I still possess a *church drawing* created at four years old. You know, way back in the day when there was no children's church and we had to sit still on a hard pew for an hour? My sketch was an entire family dressed for church; Dad with hat, suit, and tie; Mother with cleavage, pearls, high heels, and Bible in hand (of course); two precious little girls dressed in their Sunday best, and as an extra, our poodle Buffy!

I saw the details, even from that young age. I believe you are either born with that gene or not.

My family has never let me live down a declaration of *seeing Old Glory* being planted on the moon by Neil Armstrong in 1969. Well, actually, now, in retrospect, *I may* have seen the clear patriotic flag decal placed on the back passenger window of our Chevrolet Impala instead of the real thing.

Along with the *seeing things gene* also came the gift of a vivid imagination!

In my defense, my stories weren't *always* a figment of my imagination.

There was also the time I saw a lion on the beach in St. Augustine, Florida. At seven, I was walking down the beach with my best friend and heard a loud roar. Of course, I followed the noise until I located the culprit: a fully maned jungle lion in the cage-fronted garage of a neighbor's beach house.

Thankfully, this did strengthen my believability after the *flag-on-the-moon* debacle.

Years passed, and as my imagination grew, so did my love for photography.

As a university art major, my favorite subjects were architecture, landscapes, still life—but most of all, people. By the time my children were born, I was locked in as the *family photographer*. It didn't pay well and, sadly, kept me from being in most of the photographs. This is a great regret. Mamas, make sure you're not always *behind the lens*!

Thankfully, for our bank account, digital photography came onto the scene. This, social media, and better yet, cell phone photography, offered moments that could be captured and shared in a second.

In the spring of 2018, my life took an unexpected turn after posting a photograph on my Facebook page. This iPhone photograph actually changed the course of my entire life. However, before we wade into the details of *that* story, *this* one must be told.

BACK IN THE SADDLE AGAIN

Three years following my divorce, upon the urging of friends *(and against my better judgment)*, I enrolled in an online dating service. If you haven't ever visited some of these sites and you need a good laugh, I highly recommend it!

The characters were many, and the possibilities few. I scrolled through endless pages of men clad in dingy wife-beater undershirts perched on top of a Harley (which was probably not even theirs). There were also the classic shots snapped in front of a dimly lit public restroom mirror. Seriously, you can't make this up! I have decided in my next life I am going to write a tutorial on what pictures *not* to post on a dating site. It truly is unbelievable. Some guys put twenty pictures of twenty different poses of only themselves. Note: Guys, at least *borrow* a friend or two for a pic so we won't all assume that you are a psychopath!

I was actually *on my way off* the site when I noticed a very different photograph.

The man on this profile wasn't smiling. He had a rather blank look on his face, which, at first, bothered me, but there was something about his eyes and *what was behind them* that caught mine. It was an original piece of art...*very contemporary*. The art intrigued me even more. His profile was well-written. It was extremely different from any of the other ones I had read. It was written in almost a riddle form and seemed worth investigating.

At this point, I had only been on the site for two weeks and had responded to several *likes* on my page. Many were handsome and *seemed* nice at first, which drew me in; that is, until they took a quick detour down a road on which I did *not* wish to travel. I was definitely not getting positive vibes about this *trendy* dating method.

Most conversations revealed exaggerated accomplishments, arrogance, neediness, or worse, rude sexual innuendos.

One *charming suitor* even asked me to move to Germany, of course, after requesting me to send money for his poor mother (insert eyeball roll).

My first conversation with this stoic man was anything *but* the above. I found him to be kind, open, courteous, and extremely intelligent, but never condescending. We were both very open about our *stories,* which had some similarities that gave us common ground.

Although nice, there were some *huge* differences. First of all, he was a *Romanian physicist.* Yes, you heard me correctly.

Not only had I never met anyone from Romania, but the closest thing to a physicist I knew was Dr. Emmett Brown on *Back to the Future*! *What could an interior designer and Romanian physicist ever have in common?*

God sure does have a sense of humor because guess what else? He was a *vegetarian!* I will admit this huge difference not only cracked me up but it also made me extremely skeptical. I am a chef and a carnivore to the core. The idea of how this could ever work was beyond me, but for some reason, I was intrigued and waded in.

After several texts and phone conversations, we decided to meet in person. He had a thick accent, which I loved, and was very polite. He insisted that we meet at a public place of my choosing for lunch where I would feel comfortable. I suggested we meet at a nearby Vietnamese restaurant, which would be well-suited for both of us.

When I arrived, he stood and extended his hand, greeted me with a kind smile, and pulled my chair out for me. Thankfully, he wasn't wearing a wife-beater, nor did he arrive on a rented Harley, so I immediately felt comfortable and sensed I had nothing to fear.

Full disclosure: *My sister was on high alert and standing by with a secret code word* and *a baseball bat in the event I suspected him to be an* axe *murderer.*

THE GENTLE MAN

Three hours later and after a few inches of snow, which unbeknownst to us had accumulated, we walked to our cars and said our goodbyes. My windshield was covered with a fresh blanket of snow. Although neither of us had a scraper, he quickly cleared it with his bare hands and offered to follow me home. That, oddly enough, was also a detail I did not dismiss lightly. I was *not* accustomed to these types of gestures and left with gratitude for his kindness.

We were vastly different in our backgrounds of faith, political views, and customs, but I was very drawn to his kind, respectful, and generous spirit. He was real in every way.

I had spent my entire life looking for *Southern gentlemen* while not always discerning and vetting out a real *gentle man*. There is a huge difference.

All this aside, I honestly don't think I would have *ever* responded to his initial *like* on my page had I not spotted that painting behind him on his. *Again...back to the details.*

Astonishingly, he seemed to possess *both* sides of the brain, which is most uncommon for a physicist. To further his education and to provide a better future, his family fled communist Romania and immigrated to the US in 1979. They settled in Chicago, where his father worked as an engineer and his mother owned and ran a small art and antique gallery. This explained his love of art. With a doctorate from Purdue, his parents clearly expected academic excellence; however, they wisely *schooled* him in many other subjects, making him passionate about not only his field of study but also in the fine arts *and travel.*

Which finally leads us to *the rest of the story.*

THE MAIDEN VOYAGE

As we continued getting to know one another, I found his life story fascinating. Learning about his customs and traditions, and even his vegetarian dishes, was so very interesting to me. Bottom line, I found him to be exactly who he had seemed to be: a very warm, kind, and generous man. Although he may not have been my *forever one*, he *was* exactly the one I needed at that critical time in my life to begin my healing process.

On Valentine's Day, he invited me to dinner, which he had prepared at his house by the lake. He had gone to so much trouble for me, making every detail special. One detail that I did not understand was a calendar of Italy tucked under my napkin. A self-declared *noticer*, I asked its meaning. He explained he was involved with a travel club and had been planning a trip to *Italy* in May, then asked if I would like to join him.

I am certain my jaw dropped at the mention. Italy had forever been at the top of my bucket list but was yet another unfulfilled dream.

He immediately set my mind at ease by saying there were no expectations or strings attached but that *he wanted to see my eyes the first time I saw the wonders of that country*. He also added if I needed to talk with my sons first *or* ask someone to go with us, he absolutely understood.

I giggled and reminded him I was fifty-three and didn't need a chaperone *or anyone's permission*; however, I did appreciate this thoughtful consideration.

Three months later, I joined him and now understand what is meant by the following statement.

Sharing places of wonder with others brings such joy.

He watched my eyes fill with tears as I stood in awe at the feet of David in Florence.

He heard my gasp as we rounded the corner and was rendered speechless at the sight of the black and white striped marble spires of the great cathedral in Siena.

He quietly watched as the most unforgettable sunset rushed through the western archway in Monteriggioni and bathed my life with inexplicable joy, the moment when Italy captivated my soul and placed a promise ring on my empty finger.

On May 31, 2018, I snapped the picture that graces the cover of this book. Although I cannot describe what occurred in that moment, *my life* is *now proof of that epiphany.*

Later that evening, I posted the picture to my Facebook page. Within moments, a friend and former client responded, "I will pay you to take me where you are right now." The following morning, I was awakened by *ten other private messages saying exactly the same thing.*

Life's lessons have taught me many things, the least of which is this: *God is the God of details. There are* no *coincidences. Pay close attention to them. They might just change your life forever.*

He used a man, the stern-looking physicist standing in front of interesting art, to pry open the closed and broken places of my heart; this man remains a treasured friend to this day.

He provided him as yet another conduit for *rediscovering my joy*.

It's all *in the details.*

THE MOMENT I MET PAOLA AND RICCARDO
IN FLORENCE AT THE MERCATO CENTRALE.

CHAPTER 3

It Takes a Village

Life is not beautiful because of the things we see or do.
Life is beautiful because of the people we meet.

—SIMON SINEK

After the big *aha* moment in the archway of
Monteriggioni in 2018, I knew if my plans in Italy were
going to materialize, there was a lot of work to be done.
Fortunately, the least of my concerns was finding clients
to go; they were actually calling me. The biggest task at
hand was finding the place, determining if it was financially
sound, making the plans, and seeing them to fruition; or
"fruitation," as my friend *Sarge Marge* says.

At the time, I was working on two design projects in
Alabama: an extensive two-year ground-up residential
in Guntersville and a large commercial renovation in
Huntsville. I spent many nights online in between these and
my daily responsibilities in Nashville, looking for the perfect
place in Italy to call *home*.

Part of that search was contacting Emily Woodroof,

director of Lipscomb University's Florence Study Abroad Program. She had lived in Italy for seven years, and I knew it was wise to have an American contact if needed, especially one like Emily!

I was intent on landing in Chianti, which is the *original* wine country and central to the places I wished to offer in my plan. I wanted a vineyard and, of course, a fabulous view. Clean and quaint, mixed with unmitigated Tuscan charm. Top of the list; it needed to be authentic, both the farm *and the owners*.

The *off-the-beaten-path* photographs from my initial trip were what drew clients to it immediately. There are millions of tours offered in Italy, but my goal was to offer a boutique experience of *living in Italy*.

I spent hours perusing websites and communicating with owners of picturesque villas, bed-and-breakfasts, and agriturismo (independently owned farms that offer accommodations).

Although there were many to choose from, I detected overly exaggerated descriptions, which concerned me. After spending nearly two months of searching, I realized the *only* failproof way to find the right place was to find it in person. *A return trip would* have *to be made*.

CALLING IN THE CAVALRY

My work schedule would definitely be a factor in planning my return, not to mention my monthly budget, *and* I would need someone to accompany me. *But who?*

After Christmas, I called one of my best friends in

Huntsville and said, "Hey Andrea, what would you think about going to Italy with me...next month?"

Now, I have to add this is my friend who boarded a plane with me in 2008 headed to Guatemala to inspect the factory that would be manufacturing my bags when I first started Haul Couture.

Andrea is my adventure-taking, thrill-seeking, fun-loving friend who is usually in for whatever crazy thing I might have up my sleeve, and I am known to pull those out fairly regularly!

With no hesitation and with the blessing of her husband, she jumped in; flights were booked, and our Italian adventure was planned. Although her jump-in attitude was great, that isn't the *best* thing about her.

The best thing is that Andrea believes in me, supports me, and encourages me. *She always has my back.*

FIND YOUR ANDREA

If I can give you some good advice, it is this: *Find* your *Andrea. Find good friends.* I sure have. These friends have been with me through thick and thin and are too many to number. Many of them are reading this book, and *all* of them encouraged me to write it.

Although I do not remember much about the traumatic night I left home after my twenty-nine-year marriage was over, I do remember arriving at one friend's home, curling up into a ball with my head in her lap. I will never forget her tears as they fell on my head. She never said a word; she just held on and cried *with* me.

I have had friends and family who have helped me move five times, paid my electric bill when times were tight, taken and sent me on trips, and sat with me through the night when I was too sick to walk.

I have had investors who lost investments because I was forced to close the business. I have had doctors and dentists who treated me, knowing I had no insurance. I have had clients who created parties to create work for me. *Oh, so many dear ones in my village.*

Returning to my hometown after thirty years brought out more of my *villagers.* I've been reunited with many childhood and college friends who have been such an encouragement to me.

Eight high school buddies showed up at my son's rehearsal dinner, aproned and ready to serve a sit-down Italian dinner for seventy-five guests, all because they love me.

I am so thankful for my *Steel Magnolias,* who have each gone through their own brush with hell. Time flies when we are together, and it is always filled with laughter, life updates, and plenty of recounted memories spent in good old Harding Hall or at Captain Anderson's in Panama City!

I could go on and on. But you get the point. *These are forever friends.*

It is more than ironic that Michael W. Smith sat in my Italian kitchen singing *Friends are Friends Forever.* Not a coincidence. I am certain that it was a little nudge from the Father reminding me to be grateful for the bounty of friends He has placed in my life.

I'm telling you, folks, it not only takes a village to raise a child...it also takes a village to survive in this terribly difficult adult world.

I am so thankful for my village. It is a wonderful one that reaches far and wide, and *it keeps growing!*

TO MARKET, TO MARKET

When we arrived in Milan in March 2019, we hopped in our rental car and headed to Florence. You may ask, "Were you nervous about driving in Italy?" Of course, but as Simon Sinek says, *Panic causes tunnel vision. Calm acceptance of danger allows us to more easily assess the situation and see the options*. With GPS in hand and Andrea as my trusty travel companion and navigator, we were ready to conquer Rome! (Well, not quite, but it reads well!)

As soon as we arrived in Florence, we checked into our hotel, then met Emily for dinner. I am not sure she ate a bite, given all the questions I threw at her. I was so grateful for this friend and her expertise.

Emily was usually involved with students during the week and traveling with them on the weekends, but fortunately, they were on a *free-travel* break, so I invited her to accompany us the next morning in Firenze (Florence). Thankfully, she obliged.

After dinner, we settled into our beautiful little hotel near the Arno and drifted off, dreaming of our Italian adventure, which awaited.

Emily's apartment was around the corner, so she met us

after breakfast, and we headed to the Mercato Centrale.

Travel tip: I've always made it a point to begin my trips with a visit to the local market wherever I travel; it is an immediate connection with the people, their customs, and of course, their culinary treats! As we drove down into the belly of the Mercato, the postage-stamp reality of this country set in as I parked in a tee-tiny spot. After regaining a pulse, we ascended into the heavenly realm of *Storico Mercato Centrale Firenze*.

LOVE AT FIRST SIGHT

It was a cold day in March, and tourists were few, but the market was still brimming with excitement, especially for these two Southern gals!

Colorful flowers, fresh fruits and vegetables of every variety, hanging cured meats, swordfish flying in the air, and octopus tentacles swirling around behind the glass. Every single part of a chicken known to mankind, huge cheese wheels, biscotti, and, of course, delicately hand-made pastas of every shape and variety were on display. However, the most celebrated star on this stage was Italy's *liquid gold*! Their pride and joy: olive oil!

As we rounded the corner at the very end of the row, I spotted a warmly lit and beautifully decorated little booth with a huge selection of olive oil. Standing in front was a petite lady dressed in a bright red puffy jacket with a fashionable scarf tied around her neck, alongside who I supposed to be her husband, donning a navy-blue wool cap with a stylish kicked-up collar. Their inviting smiles definitely made them stand out in the crowd.

She greeted us with the typical Italian kiss-kiss...left cheek, then right. *That* is how it is done, and *I adored it*!

Their booth was stacked from floor to ceiling with Italy's finest treasures; Olive oil of every size and flavor; Chianti, Grappa, flavored local honey, pesto and balsamic vinegars, kitchen gadgets, and olive wood products. They sell everything you could imagine to fill an Italian gift basket.

Although Paola Guercini spoke broken English, she could converse very well. Riccardo, her adorable husband, spoke very little, but with his twinkly eyes and big smile, it wasn't necessary.

As we were talking, I noticed the sign hanging above, which read: *Agriturismo Annita Poggio Alle Lame— Tavarnelle Val di Pesa.*

I was familiar with this area and had actually booked an appointment at a B and B in Tavarnelle later that week. I immediately started asking questions.

Thankfully, Emily was with us and translated a few things here and there.

Another thing you should know about me is that I usually have an immediate gut feeling about things. Outside of a few *major fails* in my life, I am typically correct about these feelings and can usually sense a good thing right away.

To say I had this feeling about Paola and Riccardo is *such* an understatement. *I seriously knew from the moment I met them they were going to be a part of my new life.*

I was beyond anxious to see the farm, but I had booked a room and planned a shopping trip in Arezzo at the famed antique market, so we journeyed south. As we passed the Tavarnelle exit, about forty minutes south of Florence, I had *that feeling*.

After two successful days in Arezzo, we returned to Tavarnelle for our appointment at the agriturismo. The first time I turned onto the long, dusty, gravel road leading to the house, I had an overwhelming sense of home. I felt as if I was returning to my grandmother's farm in Missouri. However, in great contrast, those flat, endless rows of cotton and soybeans were replaced by rolling hills etched with twisted vines and olive trees.

There is also something about the sky and clouds in Tuscany. It seems bluer, clouds fluffier, sunsets more vibrant, and the atmosphere clearer. Perhaps, it is because I was seeing it with unfiltered eyes and an open heart.

AGRITURISMO ANNITA: MY NEW HOME AWAY FROM HOME

The farm exudes Italian warmth, charm, and authenticity. These qualities are seen not only in the surroundings of Annita but also in the beautiful family that has occupied it for well over a century.

The farm has been in Paola Guercini's family for over five generations. Note: In Italy, the wife retains her maiden name; the children take the surname of their father.

A tradition of excellence has been passed down on this farm where both award-winning Chianti and olive oil are produced. This is clearly evident after the first sip of their DOCG Chianti. DOCG, literally translated, means *Controlled and Guaranteed Denomination of Origin.* It is the highest classification Italian wines can be awarded and can be seen on the neck of every hand-filled bottle. There are a little over seventy such DOCGs in Italy.

When Paola was a little girl, her grandfather would send her in to wash the giant oak barrels between seasons. These barrels still reside in the cantina beneath my apartment. They, along with century-old olive jars, are sitting in the same undisturbed spot they have occupied for generations.

A renovation project of this hidden gem, the original cantina, took place on my visit in the spring of 2020 and is now a fascinating addition to this working farm. Photographs and artifacts beautifully illustrate the story of these people, whom now I call *famiglia.*

The barn, which is over three hundred years old, is the oldest structure on the farm and was renovated into three guest apartments in 2005. These *apartments* are not typical by American standards. Each has been beautifully appointed with Paola's family antiques, respectfully retained. Vaulted ceilings with original beams, softly faded stucco walls, and exquisitely handcrafted ironwork accent this perfect example of simple Tuscan living.

The view of the vineyard from the bedroom window of the Belvedere is unparalleled at sunset.

Riccardo Paolella not only owns, manages, and runs the farm but did most of the renovations himself. This talented farmer, also a master blacksmith like his father, did all the ironwork in each apartment and in the main house.

A HUG AND A HANDSHAKE

If I had given God a checklist of what I was searching and praying for, *this was it*. Each and every detail was e*xactly* what I had dreamed of, not only for my guests but also for me. I would be spending nearly three months away from home, so my living space and connection with the host family were very important.

Thankfully, Emily Woodroof was available to meet us at the farm. I knew having her there would be invaluable. She knows the language, customs, and what to expect. After the tour, negotiations began. Again, every single detail was exactly what I had been looking for.

With a hug, kiss, handshake, *and a toast with their Chianti*, my Italian dream became a reality.

LA MIA FAMIGLIA

The loss of *the village* into which I married was the greatest loss and has been one of the most difficult obstacles to navigate.

I now realize that longing to be a part of *that village* actually factored into marrying at such a young age. I adored my mother- and father-in-law and totally anticipated that my life would mirror theirs: *happily ever after*. Unfortunately, some things just don't quite work out as we have planned.

I still love that family, and although I do maintain a relationship with them, it will never be the same. It cannot be.

One quiet evening (*which is rare during harvest*) during my second season, Paola and I sat in my *chicken* (what she calls kitchen) and talked about raising sons. Although our customs and traditions have their differences, our mother hearts are one and the same. We laughed and cried as we swapped tales and adventures of life as mothers of boys. That night was such a sacred time with my *sister-friend,* who is now one of the most important people in my life.

After she left, I had yet another epiphany that gave me a new perspective and healing.

In 2015 when I began those *path-placing prayers* to my Father, I never dreamed that He would be preparing yet another family for me. This family would live five thousand miles from my home in Nashville, tucked away on a humble farm in the heart of Tuscany.

What a good, good Father He is to have assembled *all* these fascinating people into my life.

Every person is a treasured part of my village...the amazing village that the Master has placed directly in my path.

2019 GUEST AT MALASPINA CASTLE IN FOSDINOVO
LOOKING OUT ACROSS THE LIGURIAN SEA.

CHAPTER 4

Vita Semplice

The greatest step toward a life of simplicity is to learn
to let go.

—STEVE MARABOLI

The first group to arrive in 2019 were the Texans.

Due to limited *boot* (trunk, not cowboy boot) space in my leased Peugeot, I placed a luggage restriction on what each guest was allowed to bring. In this tiny country, I have learned that *less is more*. The apartment also provides a wonderful little washing machine, so traveling light is made easier. I also want each guest to have ample room in their luggage to return with wonderful Italian treasures found along the way.

Well, the saying that *everything is bigger in Texas* also applies to their luggage! When my assistant Lorenzo arrived at the airport in Florence to pick them up, he had to work a little magic squeezing them *and their luggage* into the vehicle.

What ever would I do without my dear Lorenzo? I met him through Emily Woodroof, my friend in Florence. Lorenzo is an instructor of Italian at several American universities that offer study abroad programs in Florence. I hired him primarily to serve as a translator when needed, but he also assists with airport pick-up when I am detained on the farm, preparing for each group's arrival. I also love to *initiate* each group with a totally Italian greeting upon their arrival, and *Lore* could not be more perfect for the job!

While the Texans settled into their apartment, I prepared the antipasti and wine and carried it to the *terrazza*. They met me there just as the blazing Tuscan sun was beginning to set. It is a glorious view that I never take for granted.

Meanwhile, back in my *cucina*, the chicken was roasting, and pasta was boiling for the Tuscan feast to follow. As the sun disappeared, we gathered around the table. Riccardo poured Chianti Classico, grown and bottled on the farm, and glorious cello music was provided by Francesco. We all lifted and clinked our glasses, shouting, "*Salute!*" In this sweet moment, Italians, Americanos, and a lovely German couple also staying on the farm joined for a picture-perfect ending to their first *simply perfect* day in Tuscany.

THROUGH THE EYE OF THE NEEDLE

Although the Texans may have had *extra luggage*, they also exercised an *extra dose of patience* with me. Being my very first group also meant that more exploration *might* occur on their adventure, and bless their hearts, it did! I had traveled everywhere on our itinerary, but not with a crew in tow. They *saddled up* every morning with a smile on their face, ready for the adventure.

Six-foot-six Steve Cone, dubbed *Don Cone-Leone*, rode shotgun and *never* said one word about my driving, which I'm certain was tempting for this truck-and-cattle-driving Texan.

Actually, he *did* make *one* comment on the day we arrived at Castello Malaspina, a medieval castle set at the top of a daunting five-mile zig-zagged climb up the steep side of the Ligurian mountains.

The instructions, per the castle director, were to *drive through the castle walls*. Now, I had been to the tiny village of Fosdinovo before, and parking was challenging at best. Although I had very specific instructions, they sounded totally impossible based on my previous visits. *Drive through the castle gate?* These directions seemed more appropriate if arriving on horseback, but an automobile?

As I have shared before, one challenge driving in Italy is knowing what *is* and *is not centro storico*, the historical center of a town. This area, in any given town or village, is only accessible by car to those with a permit, actually living or working within its walls. *The entire village of Fosdinovo is zoned as such.*

I was determined, however, to follow Renee's instructions, so thru the gate we went. We tucked the side mirrors, and everyone sucked in as we drove through the ancient medieval gate, immediately turning into an even *more narrow path* that led to the back entrance of the castle. I literally had less than three inches on either side of the car to spare! When I finally made it through the *eye of the needle*, Steve said, "Dang girl! You are the shiz! I will go *anywhere* with you... That was some mighty fine driving!" (I may have changed the words a bit for my mother's sake)

Even with all my missed turns, thankfully, I earned my stripes with the Texans *and* a badge of courage for myself. This newfound confidence carried me through the next three months as I channeled my inner *Mario Andretti* across Tuscany. It takes a great deal of bravery *and* hutzpah to drive in Italy, and I earned it!

CASTELLO MALASPINA

The first written record of this medieval fortress dates back to 1164. It became the seat of the Marquises of Massa. The castle, found in the province of Massa Carrara, dominates a rocky hill perched on the slopes of the Apuan Alps overlooking the Tyrrhenian coast.

Malaspina Castle was expanded by Spinetta Malaspina the Great in the early 1300s. Built originally as a military fortress, Spinetta and a line of marquises transformed the castle over the next four hundred years into a residence.

Defensive elements and important building inventions were added, finally completing the work in the seventeenth century. The smooth stonework was said to have been an architectural feat and gave strength to its fortification. At the end of the nineteenth century, the complex was transformed into a prison and was used as such until 1946.

During World War II, the village of Fosdinovo was badly damaged, as the castle was occupied and used as German army headquarters. It suffered severe bombing attacks by the allied forces but was completely restored by the family in the early 1960s.

History records that *Dante Alighieri* was said to have taken refuge there in 1307 after being exiled from Florence. Accounts say the *Supreme Poet* was a regular guest at the castle and actually penned part of his *Inferno* within the walls. The only remaining original fourteenth-century fresco is located in the Dante room, which depicts a resurrected Christ and a kneeling Malaspina, who is about to depart for the Crusades.

Literary master Gabriele D'Annunzio wrote these words: "I like to think that Dante, as a guest of the Malaspina family, envisioned the City of Dis by looking at the Apuan Alps in flames at sunset, as vermillion as if they were on fire."

The amazing vista seen from his window, filled with marble-rich Alps, is clearly enough to inspire even the most exiled writer. It is magnificent.

Echoes of knight-laden horses galloping up into the stone-sloped entrance can easily be imagined within these walls...and maybe even faintly heard. There are numerous stories of *sightings and hauntings*; it takes very little imagination, but there are *no* eerie feelings in this place. I did take an interesting picture upon my second stay, which to this day does leave me baffled.

The castle is still privately owned and maintained by the Malaspina descendants. A meticulously detailed family tree is painted in the hall just outside the master dining hall, which shows descendants as far back as the late 1300s. The castle's condition truly stands today as a testament to the fortitude and resiliency of this family.

SEMPLICE

Instead of cashing in and selling it to the highest bidding *Hilton or Marriott* when times were difficult, this noble family has maintained the structure's grandeur and dignity in *semplicità* (simplicity). Time stands still in Malaspina Castle. The family is most intentional to continue things in the manner it has for centuries.

The rooms are simply and authentically appointed. You will find no phone, no television, and no air-conditioning. In fact, a letter is given to every guest, signed by the current owners, Count Pietro and Maddalena Malaspina, with a tongue-in-cheek *apology* for its simple nature. In this letter, guests are encouraged to *concentrate on themselves, abandon the distractions, and from deep within, bring to light thoughts and feelings that may have become dormant.*

I have never received any complaints from my guests. Instead, all who stayed at Malaspina counted themselves fortunate to steal away from the *distractions* for a night immersed in the history of this magical place.

Sleeping in late at the castle is not very likely as the village bells begin to peal brilliantly at 7:00 a.m., heralding a new day.

As you fling open the eight-foot wooden windows, sunlight streams into the room, and the Mediterranean breeze kisses your face. On a clear morning, panoramic views of the Tyrrhenian Sea are relished, and for a moment, you are reminded that *once upon a time*, nobles stood in these very windows drinking in this same intoxicating view.

In a few minutes, another bell sounds, this time from within the walls, and you are awakened from this mesmerizing moment and called to breakfast.

A sixteen-foot dining table in the grand dining hall or a small octagonal table located in what once was used as the kitchen is the setting for this simple Ligurian breakfast that now is laid before you. Breakfast begins with caffè and tea, then follows scrumptious local yogurt with fresh berries and seeds served with a drizzle of the most unique *smoked* honey drawn from bees buzzing in and out of the castle walls.

Fresh pears, plums, and apples picked from the castle orchard...then Italian sausages and cheeses, homemade preserves, freshly baked bread, pastries, and the *best* butter to ever cross my lips round out a filling but simple Tuscan breakfast, very indicative of this region.

After breakfast and interesting conversations about *strange noises heard in the night*, the reality of our impending road trip pushes us on as we say *ciao* to our wonderful adventure at Castello Malaspina!

VITA SEMPLICE...SIMPLE LIFE

One of the things I have come to love the most about Italy is *vita semplice*...simple life. Simple life in no way implies dull or less full. Why, the very hand gestures of the Italians display fullness and exaggeration. A grand life can indeed be a simple one.

I do believe *in these simple moments, life can be experienced and savored to the fullest.*

One wouldn't look at this grandiose fortification and think of the word *semplice*. However, it is within these massive, medieval walls that the idea of *less is more* is so well displayed.

I quote from the letter given to guests by Count Pietra Malaspina...

> As with the divine Michelangelo, who also used to frequent the nearby mountains, who was able to give form to his masterpieces by chiseling away the excess from a block of marble so that the form that for him the stone already contained could be revealed, we also believe that the art of removal is an extraordinary way to add that something that is missing from our lives.
>
> Vita semplice.

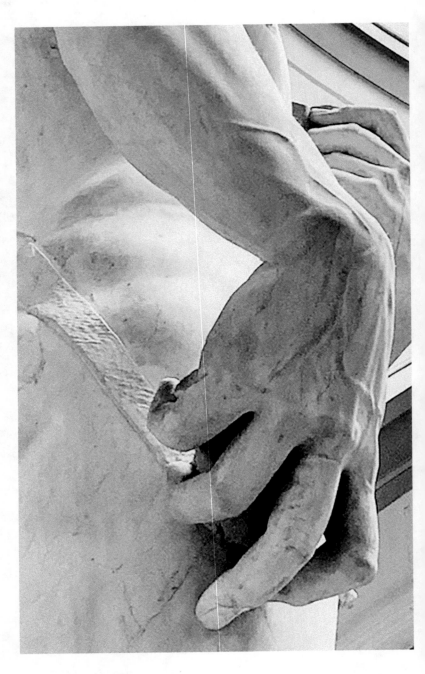

HIDDEN STONE CLENCHED IN MICHELANGELO'S DAVID'S HAND.

CHAPTER 5

"Draw What You See, *Not* What You *Think* You See"

Never lose an opportunity of seeing anything beautiful, for beauty is God's handwriting.

—RALPH WALDO EMERSON

"Draw what you see, *not* what you *think* you see" was the first statement we heard every day as freshman art students at Lipscomb University in Nashville, Tennessee. Our classes were located in *The Dungeon*, the basement of Sewell Hall (the oldest men's dorm on campus). Every day, we hopped up on wooden stools, flipped open our large sketch pads, and immediately had our attention directed to a solid white marble bust of *David* which sat in the center of the classroom.

While most other university students across the country were studying the entire body of *Michelangelo's David*, on this Christian campus, we were given the *shoulders-up, G-rated* version. As we arrived, we knew the drill. We were instructed to sketch the bust: one day with pencil, another with pastel, and another with charcoal. Every day a new exercise. Every day becoming more familiar with this historic and most beloved Renaissance sculpture.

I remember gazing into *David's* deep, stern eyes and following his muscular jawline down his perfectly chiseled neck. I remember loving the assignment of drawing his billowy locks. He was a dream to draw *and* to dream about. *Draw what you see,* not *what you* think *you see.* I can safely say that by the end of my freshman year, I knew *David's* face more intimately than any other man in my life, *and* I had developed an enormous mythical crush on him.

One fall morning, several weeks into the semester, we arrived to find bandanas laid across each of our drawing boards. That day we were challenged to sketch *David* completely blindfolded.

I loved the exercise and will never forget it. As I drew, I imagined myself standing in the Accademia in Florence, gazing up at this beautiful man and dreaming of the day I would meet him in person.

REVIVING A LOST LOVE

In May 2018, just before leaving for my first trip to Italy, I climbed the wobbly pull-down stairs of my attic to retrieve my luggage. As I was maneuvering my suitcase down the steps, my eye caught an old friend. I spotted my *ancient* brown portfolio, dusted it off, and carefully unzipped the zipper. To my surprise, tucked safely away from the ravages of time were my old sketches of *David*.

My mind immediately reflected on those carefree days

in college. I recalled friends and colleagues who sat on the stools with me. Many have enjoyed successful art careers: Anna Japp, Harold Krauss, and Michael Shane Neal, just to mention a few.

Others used their degree in different ways, as I did. Although our studio was a humble one and very underfunded, we were fortunate to study under some extremely gifted instructors.

As I continued to flip through the memories, at the bottom of the stack was my *blindfolded David*. The words echoed, *Draw what you see,* not *what you* think *you see.* As I pondered, my heart began racing at the very thought of seeing him in person!

Just as I will never forget those college memories, I will also *never* forget the first time I stood in the *Galleria dell'Accademia* in Florence at the feet of this magnificent sculpture and wept. That moment will be forever chiseled upon my heart, and I will *never* be released from its spell.

The sheer massiveness of *David* is enough to leave you speechless. How could it even be possible that a man of twenty-six years could turn a raw piece of Carrara marble into such a masterpiece? It is exquisite in form, matter, and composition. The history behind its creation is also beyond comprehension.

Michelangelo actually inherited the unfinished project of Agostino di Duccio and Antonio Rossellino.[1] Both sculptors rejected the enormous block of marble due to the

---

1 Accademia.org, "Michelangelo's David," accesed April 27, 2023, https://www.accademia.org/explore-museum/artworks/michelangelos-david.

presence of too many *taroli* (imperfections), which may have threatened the stability of such a huge statue. It had been abandoned and neglected for twenty-five years (the entirety of Michelangelo's life) when he was commissioned to finish the piece for the Cathedral of Florence. The Vestry Board had established a religious subject for the statue but never expected the revolutionary interpretation as it was created. He worked tirelessly for over two years to create one of the most breathtaking masterpieces known to the modern world.

Although I studied this work in Art History, there were so many details of the statue that I am embarrassed to admit I missed.

As I slowly made my way around the enormous sculpture, I soaked in every detail as if breathing him in.

To my astonishment, I discovered the slingshot elegantly draped over his muscular back, and then, as I followed it, I discovered *the vein*. It is as if you can see the blood pumping through the bulging vein in his hand...absolutely stunning. How could a *real* art major ever have missed that detail? I decided this discovery was actually a gift reserved for the day we finally met.

Upon closer study, I also found the stone, which took the life of Goliath, tightly clenched in his hand. This, too, was very symbolic, and I tucked it away as another gift of relevance to my present life.

Every visit with new clients reveals yet a new appreciation for what is obviously called the greatest sculpture of all time. *I dare* anyone *to challenge that statement.* There is a hushed sense of reverence as you enter the hallway, paying respect to the artist *and* the art.

I cry *every* time I step onto the marble *runway* of the long gallery where this glorious piece of art resides. I cry not only because of the magnitude of what I am seeing but because God allowed me to see it and so generously provided the way for me to do so. Little did I know the bigger plan for *David* and me—one beyond my wildest dreams.

REFLECTIONS

As I connect this story of my past with the present, I see many applicable lessons that can be drawn from that statement made to the group of college freshmen. *Draw what you see,* not *what you* think *you see.*

After a life filled with both triumphs *and* tragedies, here are two obvious ones.

First, see things as they really are, not what you have *dreamed them to be.*

I am not trying to be a *Debbie Downer*, but looking at life through rose-colored glasses might not always serve you as well in the long run as a good dose of reality will. *Rose-colored glasses can hide the deepest thorns.*

Secondly, look for and focus on the beautiful things. Be present and thankful for the insignificant, everyday blessings that the Master Artist has created for us to enjoy. *We tend to focus on the mess while completely missing the masterpiece!*

Today, I am going to be the art instructor and challenge

you to do something. This assignment will not require a sketch pad, a pencil, or a blindfold. Close your eyes. On the beautifully created blank canvas of your mind, *draw what you see*, not *what you* think *you see*.

See a bright yellow daffodil grasped in the tiny hand of a child. The sun's blinding rays as it dances across the edge of the sea at sunset. Look into the cloudy but wisdom-filled eyes of your aging parents. Stand in awe at the base of a snow-covered mountain.

Taste the nectar of a Chilton County peach as it drips down your chin or salty butter as it melts on a piping hot cathead biscuit straight from the oven or a refreshing glass of freshly squeezed lemonade on a hot August day.

Smell the earthy aroma of freshly ground beans as they are being prepared for the perfect cup of coffee or the unmistakable scent of linens hung out to dry under the hot summer sun.

Feel the first silky curl of a baby or bask in the warmth of a sun-warmed car in the middle of a winter day. Simply enjoy the gift of hot water under the steady stream of your shower at the end of a long, hard day.

Listen with excitement to the rapid heartbeat of an unborn child for the very first time. Close your eyes and drift away to the drone of a bow as it is slowly pulled across the strings of a cello.

Life is *so* beautiful. *See it, taste it, smell it, feel it, hear it.* Be thankful for it *all*. It will not last long.

Draw what you see, not *what you* think *you see.*

MY BEAUTIFUL FRIEND, GIANNA ON THE DAY WE MET.

CHAPTER 6

Up, Up, and Away

You are to pay special attention to those who, by accidents of time, or place, or circumstances, are brought into closer connection with you.

—SAINT AUGUSTINE

A cool breeze stung my face as I opened the heavy iron door at the foot of the stairwell that led up to my apartment. Running at 6:00 a.m. was not a regular habit for me, but due to our early departure, *and* my concentrated effort to *ward off the carbs* of this country, I decided to make a run for it!

My typical route at home consists of a two-mile jaunt around the neighborhood. If I am being completely honest, it is usually met with resistance, but nevertheless, I have tried to add it to my daily to-do list.

Running on a gravel road in the heart of the Chianti is not a *to-do* but rather a *get-to-do*! I find myself running without ever even glancing at my watch or verifying the distance; I just run. It is an immense buffet for the senses.

Sights...rolling hills dotted with Cypress trees and billowy white clouds, a veritable watercolor before your eyes.

Sounds...roosters crowing, calm breezes blowing, and in the distance, a tractor making its way down a long, dusty vineyard row...All while being enveloped in a muted, peaceful silence.

Smells...rosemary, sage, lavender, and the faint smell of fruit-laden olive trees. However, the best smell of all to this Missouri-born girl is the intoxicating scent of *earth*...the rich soil in which the harvest is now growing.

As I have noted, one of my favorite things about Italy is literally *breathing*. I breathe intentionally, deeply...*all the way*.

On this beautiful morning, just as I was rounding the corner of the villa, I heard an unfamiliar sound. A huge burst of air, almost like the fiery breath of a dragon. This sound was clearly not something I experienced on a regular basis, but I am in Italy, and anything is possible. To my astonishment, I looked up, and instead of a dragon, there was an enormous hot air balloon flying about twenty feet above my head!

My heart leapt as I watched it slowly make its ascent into the brilliant blue sky. I quickly ran back into the casa, up the stone staircase, and frantically knocked on Paola's door. "Paola, come quickly! Now!"

As we descended the stairs, I tried to explain what I had seen. Once outside, we stood arm-in-arm, looking up in wonder, giggling with the excitement of two teenaged girls.

I had been wanting to add this experience to my guest's itinerary since my arrival but had been unsuccessful, partially due to my busy schedule, also perhaps to miscommunication between Paola, Riccardo, and me. When I asked them about it, they knew about a nearby business but were unsure if it was still open. Something had *happened*, and I abandoned my search.

After making a call to Lorenzo, my assistant, the company information was easily found. We discovered the company was actually located less than two miles from our farm in Tavarnelle Val di Pesa *and* open for business.

I called Gianna Volpi, the owner, and began a conversation with her. She was kind but reserved. She spoke perfect English, but there was something *odd*. I couldn't quite put my finger on it. Again, possibly a communication issue, as is often the case.

After a few days, our first group was scheduled for a flight. We were to arrive at 6:15 a.m. sharp.

Upon arrival, the sun was just starting to peek over the surrounding mountains, and a chilly fog laid a heavy blanket over the ground. With nervous excitement, we entered the basket and were given instructions; fire ignited, weights were cut, *dragon's breath* sounded, and we were off.

Although there are no adequate words to fully describe this adventure, I will attempt.

It is a blend of excitement *and* nervousness that transforms in an instant to complete exhilaration and weightless wonder.

I am certain there are many other beautiful places in the world to enjoy a hot air balloon excursion, but to float over the heart of Tuscany is unforgettable:

Towering cypresses that stand guard along narrow lanes. Ancient monasteries, castles, and stone farmhouses, set among endless hills planted with golden sunflowers and wheat, meticulously planted rows of olive groves, and sun-kissed vineyards.

These abstract landscapes, which have inspired the greatest renaissance painters and artists for centuries, lie before your eyes and are bathed in the dew and first light of day.

Glorious. Spiritual. Heavenly.

Although this story could have ended here, it didn't. The *rest of the story* was actually yet another prodding in the writing of this book.

After a gentle landing in a nearby field, we were picked up and driven to the country estate of Gianna, the balloon company owner. We were graciously welcomed and treated to a typical Italian breakfast. Although the food may have been *typical,* this moment would be *anything but.*

As we gathered around her perfectly appointed table filled with local fruits, freshly baked croissants, cheeses and meats from the area, Italian coffee, and, of course, Prosecco, Gianna came out of the stone house and quietly sat down beside me.

She was tall, slender, and exquisitely beautiful. I did, however, sense a certain fragility. She looked intently at me through her big, black Italian sunglasses and asked, "Kimberly, what is your story?"

I laughed under my breath and said, "Well, do you want the

long or short version?" Again, she quietly replied, "Your *story*."

I have become hesitant to answer this question. Mostly because I no longer wish to be *defined* by my story. I am finally to the point where I want to be known more for the *refined* part of it. Still, I knew that she was probing for a reason, so I answered.

"Well, Gianna, my husband of nearly thirty years decided he wanted to be with someone other than me...actually, a man other than me." This is typically a mic drop.

She lowered her head, looked down at her hands, then slowly lifted them to her face. She removed her sunglasses, exposing tear-filled eyes, and replied, "Kimberly, my husband of thirty years did not wake up two months ago."

Another mic drop...but this one, for me.

At that moment, two women from different countries, cultures, and lives were *instantly* connected. We had a bond that only surviving deep pain and immense sorrow could produce. Although our losses were distinctly different, they were the same. *Fear, loneliness, sadness, and uncertainty.*

We stood, embraced, and walked arm in arm to the edge of her terrace, which had a sweeping view of the olive grove that was beautifully lit by the morning sunrise. Both, for a moment, lost in memories from lives past, we said nothing but held on to each other as new confidants, sisters, and friends.

With an emptiness, she turned and asked, "How did you learn to breathe again?"

My answer to this question came quickly. "My faith, family, and friends."

Without a pause, she replied, "What do you do if you have no faith?"

My heart sank. I did *not* have an easy answer for this. So, for a moment, we just stood there, still, silently staring out into the distance. I thought. I prayed. I waited. *Oh, God, please give me the right answer...please help me say the right thing.*

"Well, Giana, when you have no faith...I guess you hope *life* sends someone to you who does. Maybe that someone is me."

VIA POGGIO ALLE LAME, TAVARNELLE, ITALY.

CHAPTER 7

God Bless the Broken Road

The trip is never too hard if you know you're going home

—THE CHOFETZ CHAIM

Finding affordable housing in Nashville has become similar to a house search in LA! The word is over a hundred people are moving into the city every day. If traffic is an indication, I believe that estimation.

When I returned home, I wanted to be in my old stomping ground, which at the time, was also close to my parents, so I began my search there. I would need to rent until I secured a job and was absolutely floored by real estate prices.

I enlisted the help of an old friend who just happened to be one of Nashville's top realtors. Based on my budget, she gave a grim outlook for finding anything in the area. Nevertheless, I continued to cruise the neighborhood of my youth. I was confident God would provide exactly what I needed, *and* in that very location.

One afternoon, I discovered a lovely little brick Tudor that appeared to be empty. It was a stone's throw away from the campus and home where I had spent over half of my life. I could actually hear the crack of the ball hitting a bat on Ken Dugan Field, which also stirred up plenty of happy memories.

The house was darling, but the curb appeal was not what made it stand out. What caught my eye was its unkept appearance on an otherwise manicured street. There was also no sign. Being the *Show Me State* girl from Missouri, I jumped out of the car, walked up to the front window, and peered through the narrow slats of the blinds. It was hard to make out, but the living room walls appeared to be painted black and were completely covered with graffiti! It was completely baffling and certainly unexpected in this Green Hills neighborhood.

Perplexed, I walked around back, peeking in to get a better look. I was determined to figure out what was going on. I called Maria and gave her the address.

She searched and reported that it wasn't currently on the market. She also told me, ironically, she sold it several years ago to a young architect who purchased it for investment purposes. Before I knew it, Maria pulled into the driveway with a key in hand. *There is a reason she is a top seller!*

FIXER-UPPER

The front room *was* indeed painted with black chalk paint. Graffiti and profanity were written on every wall as well as on many wooden doors and baseboards. The kitchen had been remodeled but was filthy and wrecked. The main bathroom had been flooded and stripped down to the studs. Most of the hardwood floors were ruined. The list went on and on.

Most people would have seen it and bailed. *I, however, knew this was my house.* Its condition was the very thing that drew me to it. I needed to create and restore. I'm pretty sure there is a counseling session wrapped up in that need of mine.

Although I didn't know its story, I knew the new story was going to include me. With my design expertise and a small crew, I knew I could transform the mess into a masterpiece. By nine o'clock that night, I had sketched every room and had implemented a plan.

Maria scheduled a meeting with the owner at ten o'clock the following morning. When he pulled into the driveway, he jumped out of the car and said, "War Eagle!" How did he know that? Now, in the South, it's a pretty good assumption that if you have an Alabama tag, it is gonna be one team or the other. I am sure the tiger-eye bumper sticker was a dead giveaway. It was also a nice icebreaker.

I chuckled, and *War Eagled* back. We exchanged small talk and walked into the house.

While walking, he said, "I think I have one of your Haul Couture bags."

I light up when a total stranger makes this comment. I inquired where it had been purchased. He explained that he had stopped in Cullman, Alabama, at an architectural antiques store one day on his way to Auburn.

"Do you know my friend Garlan Gudger?" I asked.

My friend, Alabama senator Garlan Gudger, owns *Southern Accents*, one of the South's finest architectural antiques stores. Actually, it is one of the best in the country. During my *Haul Couture* days, Garlan asked me to design a custom bag for the store. I was so excited to see it again and was thrilled for us to make this connection.

He continued by saying that he *looked me up* and knew all about *Haul Couture*.

We eventually moved from that conversation to the subject at hand. Maria worked her magic and devised a plan that would be mutually beneficial; I would handle the renovation and, in return, get a greatly reduced rental rate. We shook hands and sealed the deal.

As he walked out the door, he turned, handed me his business card, and asked me to come by his office for a *visit* on Monday. *Unknown to me...my new boss had just walked out the door.*

I took possession of the house on August 31, 2015, *what would have been my thirtieth wedding anniversary.* I took this as another *sign* and decided it would be the anniversary of my *new life in Nashville.*

On the hottest day of the year, I spent my *first anniversary* pulling weeds from the neglected flower beds... again, another nod to new beginnings. I knew at some point God would redeem this day for me, and He did.

I had approximately a month to finish renovations before starting work, so I quickly summoned a handy friend and his work crew from Alabama, and in no time, my little house was transformed into a home for me and Miss Weazy, my fourteen-year-old English cocker.

RAINY DAYS AND MONDAYS

For almost forty years, I had worked for myself. Having a boss and being totally surrounded by millennials was definitely a new hat to wear, but I was very excited and ready to be challenged. The new position required many things that were in my *wheelhouse* but was also filled with tasks unfamiliar to me. However, I jumped in head first, grateful for this new opportunity.

Hanging with the *tech side* of this young architectural firm was definitely difficult, and my job was heavy-ended in this area.

Monday morning meetings usually made me both excited about new projects *and* nervous about existing ones. These feelings provided days that swung from highest highs to lowest lows. Honestly, and now in retrospect, most of the lows were due to my own feelings of inadequacy, which sadly had become a familiar *bag* I had learned to carry.

I worked super hard to find my place within the company, and for over a year, things seemed to be headed in the right direction. However, just as I was finishing a huge project in which I had been called upon to produce, I began to sense a strained and uncomfortable feeling that had been growing between my young boss and me. Although I had become a pro at *ignoring fears and assumptions* in my

69

previous life, I could read between the lines and anticipated a storm brewing, and it was.

Two weeks before Christmas, the *storm* arrived. I received a text from my boss and was asked to meet him and the office manager at the end of the day in the conference room. My gut feelings have been honed, and I was pretty certain that this meeting wasn't going to have a happy ending.

To be fair, when I was hired, I was told, "We actually don't have a position for you, but we have a lot of work we know you will be well-suited for," and I was hired. I have always been able to spin many plates and wear many hats, and I did.

I am also certain that a huge part of my hiring was due to the neglected property, which needed to be renovated and that he wanted to sell. That task alone would make me well worth my salary. My *Pollyanna* self dove in head-first, feeling that after I was on the job...doing what I do best, they would need me enough to keep me on. I was wrong.

After thirty minutes of *small talk* and skirting around the issue, I was kindly told, "Kim, we really appreciate the great job you have done..." They even offered a part-time position, but I knew that the clock would be ticking *and* that they needed to hire new architects to keep up with the demand. I was clearly at the bottom of the totem pole and knew it would be best to leave.

To exacerbate the situation, I was informed that the rental house was also to be sold as soon as possible. House and job...both gone. Yet another blow to my newly adjusted sea legs and partially-repaired self-confidence. Outside of my divorce, I have never been *let go*. Strange and most uncomfortable feeling.

As I left the office located in the heart of East Nashville, the bottom fell out of the sky. Between tears in my eyes and the torrential rain on my windshield, I found it nearly impossible to see. I made a pit stop to let the rain ease up and to check on a booth I had rented at a local antique mall. The contents of my booth were remnants from my former life, plus flea market and estate sale acquisitions. Although it did provide a little extra income, it had become a drain on my time and energy.

After sprucing up the booth, I ran through the freezing rain to my car. Completely drenched, I opened the door, hopped in, and put my key in the ignition. *Nothing. Totally dead.*

Did I mention that it was also a Monday?

DADDY TO THE RESCUE

Thankfully, my parents lived less than a mile away, so I called my dad. I sat there waiting, sobbing, and going back down into that deep, dark hole of despair. *What more, Lord? How could You lead me here just to take it all away? Have I not been faithful enough?*

Even in rush-hour traffic, Dad arrived within ten minutes. In the deluge, he jumped-started my car, then climbed up into my passenger seat. As soon as he looked at me, he knew there was more. I have never been able to keep anything from him. He has always had a keen sense of *something going on*, and my mascara-stained face was an obvious clue.

I began to tell him about the unraveling of my day, and just as good daddies do, he assured me that everything would be okay and that it would all work out for the best. They were there and would help me. The *last* thing I wanted was to be another burden to them.

Although I did leave encouraged, I headed home, put my pajamas on, and snuggled into bed with Weazy and sobbed uncontrollably. Sometimes you just need a good cry.

It wasn't long until I heard a knock at my door. There stood my sister.

Kathryne and I have always been close, but proximity and raising kiddos had put time and space between us. She had also experienced a *dark time* of her own, but through love, counseling, and a *great village,* she came through stronger and with an extra measure of wisdom. She poured love, assurance, and compassion into me that night. Basically, she just held me, allowed me to cry, and assured me that I would get through this too.

Looking back on it now, I realize that this was just another *plan B* moment orchestrated by God to move me on to bigger and better things. At the time, it was very difficult, but I am so grateful for my time working with such a talented group of people and for the lessons I learned while there.

TOMORROW IS ANOTHER DAY FOR THE UNSINKABLE MOLLY BROWN

At this point, it needs to be noted that I have always identified with *Molly Brown*. In fact, it has been said if I had been a passenger on the Titanic, I would have commandeered a lifeboat, gathered survivors and a crew, *and* served refreshments while on our way to safety!

My inner *Unsinkable Molly Brown* was going to be fully tasked for strength and courage to weather this new storm.

After contacting my realtor and hearing her say the odds of finding another sweet deal in this area were even more remote than the first time, *Molly Brown and Scarlett O'Hara* hit the road every day, looking for something...anything.

One afternoon, I noticed a new sign that had not been there earlier in the day. I pulled into the driveway of a little brick ranch on a nearby street. I hopped out, looked through the windows, and dialed the hand-written number that was on the sign.

A very kind voice answered. When I inquired about the property, she asked for my name. She recognized my voice and told me that she was acquainted with my parents through church and actually lived on the property behind the house. Within minutes, she arrived and opened the house. It had been newly renovated...was clean as a whistle and really cute. It was small but an absolutely perfect place, even better suited for my needs than my present home. Within a week, I was packed and moving into my new home. Yet another prayer answered. *Tomorrow was another day!*

After a few restless nights, lots of prayer, *and* a few dreams, I began to see things much more clearly. It was time for me to reignite my entrepreneurial spirit and start a new business. The new name of my business was even revealed in my dream.

FLOURISH... MAKING LIFE EXTRAORDINARY.

My logo and tagline describe my business perfectly. It has a lamp, a spoon, and a quill pen. Interior design, catering/events, and writing. These are my God-given gifts, have always been a huge part of my life, and could sustain me.

After thirty years of being an interior designer, I knew that the main offering of my business would need to be design. However, since moving to Nashville, I had also taken on quite a bit of catering for friends and clients. Both of these services went hand-in-hand. Although design and events carried much weight, I also knew that writing a book would, at some point, be another part of this equation.

Just like manna from heaven, a friend and former client called. She was ready to refresh what we had done fifteen years before. It felt so good to pull out paint chips and fabric swatches and put *my own* design skills back into gear. Best of all, it felt good working directly with people again and creating special spaces perfect for their needs.

Although I was finding plenty of work, life in Nashville was expensive, and I found myself living day-to-day, many times not knowing how I would make ends meet. However, *every single time* I found myself coming up short, a new opportunity would surface, and God would provide.

One of the greatest blessings I have experienced from this *difficult time* was learning complete and total dependence on God. Although I had always been a faithful believer, I don't think I had ever totally surrendered.

I've always been a *planner, a fixer*, and I might even say a manipulator of situations. Part of these attributes are strengths, and I am thankful for the optimistic attitude that was instilled in me. I am also thankful for the non-complacent Scarlett O'Hara side of me, who is willing to rise up and find new ways to survive.

I now realize that these positive attributes can also be connected to pride, which is a weakness. It was only in complete brokenness I fully realized that although I might be a pretty decent fixer-upper, *there* is *a limit to* my *skill set.*

God's ability to fix, restore, and rebuild has no *limits.*

He will make my path both clear and more wonder-filled than anything *I might have been able to create.*

If that sounds preachy, so be it. It has been a hard truth to realize *and to realign.*

Surrender does not come easily or without a price. *It requires total faith, which trusts no matter what outcome might lie ahead, it was perfectly created by the Father,* and *it will be used for my good and for* His *purpose.*

This realization and surrender have been one of the greatest blessings of my life and one for which I am profoundly grateful.

LIVING IN THE LAND OF PLAN B

Have you ever known someone who, from the outside, seems to *have it all*? They live in a big house in the best neighborhood, drive a fancy car, don't have to work, go on fancy vacations, have the most handsome husband, and of course, all four of their children are star athletes *and* are headed to Harvard! Oh, and worst of all, *they are also the ones who sit there eating chocolate cake in their size 2 Calvin Kleins! Ugh!*

Wanna know a secret? I have discovered these folks actually live in a mansion on *plan A Street.* Although they *may seem to have it all*, they are the ones who cry over a smudged nail and lose their mind over a fender-bender. They scream on the sidelines and cannot tolerate an incorrect order at the restaurant, even when the server is in the weeds. These poor souls are *handicapped* and sadly not equipped to handle many of life's big challenges.

Well, guess what? I am fully equipped! Actually, some days I wonder why God keeps *equipping* me, but my plan is clearly not His. Letting go of my *plan A, Fixer-Upper-Joanna Gaines self has* allowed God to take over my *renovation,* which has removed *so* much of the pressure!

Learning to *intentionally* live in plan B also lessens fear and disappointment. It equips you for life's *big storms*.

Honestly, there were many days when I asked, "Why has this happened? How will I survive?" There were also days when it was difficult to see Him or hear His voice, but I *knew* He was still there, behind the fog *and* all those tears. He was *creating and planning, waiting for His perfect time.*

On *those* dreary days, never did I dream I'd be walking down a gravel road in the heart of Tuscany... *but my Father did.*

He already had plan B ready and waiting, *or was it actually plan A?*

God, *thank You* for the broken road that led me straight to You.

MY FRANCESCO "FRENCHY" PLAYING THE CELLO AT DINNER.

CHAPTER 8

Bella Musica

Where words fail, music speaks.

—HANS CHRISTIAN ANDERSEN

One of the first things packed for my first three-month stay in Italy was my Bose speaker. Time in Italy would not be complete without music wafting throughout my apartment.

The first playlist I opened was an opera mix. Luciano Pavarotti's rendition of *Nessun Dorma* filled the confines of my wonderful little casa. It was a crisp fall morning, so I threw open the wooden windows of my apartment to invite the sun in and to inhale the fall breeze sweeping across the vineyard. Outside my window, I could hear cousin Ennio singing with my Pavarotti at the top of his lungs. Music is such an international language!

Italy has long been an epicenter for classical music, and by the beginning of the twentieth century, the Italians made a universal mark with their distinct sound, which reflected their identity. I wasn't surprised to discover that the violin, cello, and piano were all invented in Italy. *Where else?*

With Italy being the seat of the Roman Catholic Church, early sacred vocal music had established deep roots that fostered other areas of music, such as *the opera,* which originated in Italy in the early sixteenth century. Giuseppe Verdi sat proudly at the helm. Other artists such as Puccini, Monteverdi, Scarlatti, Rossini, Vivaldi, Clementi, and Paganini—all Italian—wrote operas, countless symphonies, and concertos. No doubt, these artists were inspired by the ethereal beauty of this country, especially found in Tuscany. Many of their iconic works still remain at the center of Italian culture to this day.

Rare was the day that I didn't hear an Italian humming (or belting) out Rigoletto's *La donna e mobile* or the famous *O Sole Mio*!

CANTINA BOCELLI

On my maiden voyage to Italy in May 2018 with *the Romanian*, with Bocelli blasting on our radio, Alexander and I zipped down the rural road to Volterra. The scarlet-red poppies were in full bloom, and I was hanging out the window, snapping pictures almost as rapidly as Alex was driving. As we slowed down to pass through a small village, I noticed a sign that read *Cantina Bocelli.* I asked, "Where are we?" We had been relying on our GPS and were not paying much attention to the map or the names on it.

I stopped photographing long enough to open my phone and verify that we were in Lajatico. "Stop! This is the hometown of Andrea Bocelli! We must turn around."

Reluctantly, he turned the car around and allowed me to swoon. I have been a huge fan of Andrea Bocelli for years, and this was such an unexpected treat. Lajatico is literally a blip on the map, but there were several *Bocelli* businesses in this one roundabout town that were worthy of a few snapshots. I made them; then we were on our way.

Just outside the village, we passed a huge billboard with Bocelli's picture and an iron security gate with a winding road clearly leading up to the estate.

Every year, Bocelli hosts a concert at *Teatro del Silenzio*, a magnificent outdoor amphitheater built on his property, benefitting his hometown. This concert has been on my Italian bucket list, but it is in July, when I am usually in the States.

As we climbed the winding hills to Volterra, we continued feasting on the angelic voice of Andrea Bocelli. I must admit that I closed my eyes and dreamed of the day that I might meet him. Little did I know how soon and that it would actually be fairly soon. This story will come. Be patient.

MY FIRST DATE WITH GIACOMO

While the entire country of Italy is filled with an abundance of musical offerings, Lucca may tip the scales in its favor. Being the home of several music conservatories and schools also lends many opportunities.

One evening, while winding through the streets and headed back to our car, my sister's family and I heard music in the distance. We followed it down a dimly lit cobblestone street until we arrived at a small performance hall.

Although we were too late for the sold-out event, we did enjoy a private concert of our own in the street. The *outdoor acoustics* resonated across the stucco walls echoing melodious notes of the glorious classical music being played within.

How many famous artists have played inside that hall? Did Puccini perform there? And how many pilgrims, like us, have been privy to the precious gift that wafted out of the open windows into the streets of Lucca? One may never know, but you can be assured this wonderful little musical venue is now on my radar and will be revisited.

Another *brush with musical greatness* occurred here on my second planning trip in the spring of 2019. I heard Lucca was lovely, and I wanted to investigate this walled city in hopes of adding it to my guests' itineraries.

Lucca is the birthplace of Giacomo Puccini, who is revered as one of the greatest Italian opera composers who ever lived. Many music festivals are held in Lucca in conjunction with this great composer and his influence in Italy and the world.

There is a Puccini Museum and a large bronze statue of him seated in the middle of *Puccini Square*. Typically, there are musicians playing or choral groups singing around it, and of course, a constant stream of tourists taking pictures with him.

*I now know Giacomo up close and personal...*very *up close and personal.*

Before I go further with the story, one of the most frustrating things about Italians is their rules. *In Italy, it is a rule... until it isn't.* Seriously, the same goes for business hours. The sign may say, "Open 10–5." That, translated, means, "If we want to open from ten to five, we might be there; unless we aren't." You just have to adapt to this laid-back style of life and learn to embrace it.

These rules also apply to their driving. Especially with their ZTL (zona traffico limitato) signs. There may be a sign, but many times it is hidden and confusing as you see people with no ZTL stickers coming in and out, or worse, you are wedged between two cars and pushed into a zona.

One of the greatest challenges in Italy is maneuvering these ZTLs and historical centers (*centro storico*). Typically a *centro storico* is a pedestrian zone, and only cars with special permits are allowed to drive within them. In Lucca, the *centro storico* is *entirely* surrounded by the ancient wall that still exists today.

This is a very important thing to know in Lucca and is actually how Puccini and I met!

On my planning tour in the spring of 2019, as Andrea and I entered the city, before we knew it, we were on a tiny one-way street...I am certain two thousand years old! I had a gut feeling we were *not* where we were supposed to be, especially when the pedestrians were glaring at us, shaking their heads, and scowling.

Another issue is that GPS does not always work within these thousand-year-old walls and ancient streets!

Just as it seemed as if we were nearing an outside wall, I made a turn and landed smack dab in Puccini Square, face to face with Giacomo! What made matters worse was I had to inch the car around the base of this huge statue to turn around! How I wish I could have asked Giacomo for directions, but he was *stone-faced,* so I opted for help at the gelato store on the corner. In my most formal *southern Italian,* I asked for directions to the nearest gate. She rolled her eyes and looked at me, and pointed in the direction we were headed. I returned to the car, put it in drive, and drove straight ahead. Neither of us dared to glance out the side windows at pedestrians walking less than an inch beside our car as we scurried to freedom. Both experiencing a different type of car sickness, we finally found the gate and parked the car: *outside* of it!

When we checked into the hotel and recounted our *adventure* to the manager, he laughed and kindly reassured us that it was a common mistake and that he would make a call to his friend at the local police station.

After our tummies settled, we dined at a fabulous little trattoria across from the hotel, *Lucca in Tavola.* Owner Michael and his wife treated us to *the best spaghetti in Italy.* Messages and photographs proving this line the walls with the likes of De Niro, Stallone, Sting, and even *the* Pope! Michael's wife's signature *She Bass* (sea bass) absolutely melts in your mouth, as does the tiramisu. His delicious fare, warm smile, adorable accent, and service made these two wandering pilgrims feel so much better!

FRENCHY... MUSIC TO MY HEART

Musical adventures of my trips have not been limited to Firenze or the small towns and villages we visit. Every group's musical adventure actually begins on our wonderful farm in Tavarnelle.

Upon arrival, guests are welcomed to a Tuscan feast with all the trimmings. One of those *trimmings* is a private cello concert played by the nimble hands of Francesco Paolella. *Frenchy*, as we have come to know him, is the only son of Paola and Riccardo, owners of *Poggio alle Lame Agriturismo dall'Annita*.

If I had to describe Francesco in one word, it would have to be "joy."

But honestly, one word just isn't enough. I would add "dynamic," "gregarious," and "effervescent." When Francesco enters a room, you can expect laughter and electricity. Paola said that from the time he was a little boy, he had that same impact. His stature may be slight, but he leaves a huge wake wherever he goes. He lives life as passionately as anyone I have ever known.

My first meeting with *Frenchy* in the spring of 2019 was a brief one; a quick handshake, an Italian *kiss-kiss*, and off he flew to join friends at the *discoteca* in Firenze. He is the same age as my youngest son, Clay, which gives me someone to dote over while I am in Italy, and dote I do.

I usually have a pot of *zuppa* waiting on the stove, luring him into my apartment for a quick hug. Just like my sons, his heart can be won over with a bowl of soup!

I have now been dubbed as his *zia americana favorita* (favorite American aunt), a title I proudly wear.

His passion for life is especially obvious in his music, which endears him to me even more.

He has been a student of the cello since the age of ten.

In Italy, a well-rounded education involves early musical training, and his passion for the cello was evident after one year of lessons.

PLAYING FOR NONNO

One evening, after obliging his *zia americana* and playing for my guests, Francesco shared this story.

As a young boy, he would return from primary school every day to find his grandfather napping by the huge stone fireplace in the kitchen, waiting for little *Frenchy* to arrive. Nonno listened intently to every note as Francesco practiced.

One can only imagine the joy Francesco must have brought into the lives of his grandparents, yet also what a great encouragement they must have been to him.

In Italy, the family unit is exceptionally close. Two or three generations often live under the same roof, as was the case in the Paolella household. When Paola and Riccardo married, they moved into the large family home of her parents, which was also occupied by her grandparents, an aunt, and cousins.

At sixteen, Francesco's cello instructor advised that in order to progress, he needed a bigger and better instrument. Upon hearing this, his grandparents took what little money they had in savings and purchased an antique cello from a local musician.

Francesco's cello was made in 1933 in Pieve di Cento, just outside of Bologna, by master violin craftsman Luigi Mozzani. Violins made in this famous workshop have increased in value substantially, and this cello is no exception, especially since it was made during the final years of Mozzani's life.

This beautifully hand-carved cello is clearly one of Francesco's most valued possessions. This is not only due to its intrinsic value but because of the love with which it was given.

I am certain every time Frenchy draws the bow across those strings, he is reminded of moments shared between him and his beloved grandparents. It is written on his face as he plays.

The same joy is seen on the faces of his parents, Paola and Riccardo. They listen intently and are obviously transported to another place and time. They are filled with pride as they witness him express his passion for life and his family through music.

The most wonderful aspect of music in Italy is that it requires no translation.

I believe that Henry Wadsworth Longfellow may have said it best of all.

Music is the universal language of mankind.

Bella Musica!

THE OLD ORANGE FIAT

CHAPTER 9

The Old Orange Fiat

We must give more in order to get more. It is the generous giving of ourselves that produces a generous harvest.

—ORISON SWETT MARDEN

In the fall of 2019, as my sister Kathryne, her husband Calvin, and her son Ben left on the train in Firenze, my twenty-seven-year-old niece, Erin, climbed in the car and quietly cried all the way back to the farm. Saying goodbye to her family was never easy, especially since moving to Chicago several years ago to work on her master's in art therapy.

Erin was to be at a wedding in Northern Ireland two weeks after her family's departure and asked if she could stay over with me until the wedding. I was delighted to have her stay in the guestroom in my apartment. Getting an extra week in Italy with this dear niece of mine was *fabulous*!

We have always shared a special *something*. They say *a niece is the closest thing you will ever have to a daughter,* and without having a daughter of my own, it is true.

I am sure, to my sister's chagrin; Erin favors me in many ways. Hopefully, the similarities we share are some of my *better* attributes. One of these is creativity and passion for art. I love the countless times our conversations end with, "Me too!"

E also exhibits many characteristics that *I wish to emulate.* Her depth of compassion, empathy, and concern for those around her is just one reason she is such a gifted counselor.

My third group from Alabama was due to arrive the next day, and I knew they would adore Erin, and I was excited for her to meet my special friends from Alabama.

WAITING FOR THE DOCTOR'S ORDERS AT THE STARTING LINE

This was an exciting time during the season. Actually, it was *the week*. The vineyard was ripe, bursting at the seams. Twisted vines were weighted down with Sangiovese grapes ready to be picked. It was going to be a great harvest, which was such a welcome relief from the former year's thin yield.

Each day Riccardo waited with great anticipation for the *doctor's* inspection *and* permission to begin the back-breaking but exhilarating process of harvesting the vineyard.

Large pallets decked with an army of dark green bottles sat at attention just outside the cantina, anxious to be filled with this year's harvest.

Well-worn harvest baskets were stacked and ready; shiny red foil labels were stamped and printed; new corks were cut; clippers were cleaned and sharpened, while inside the cantina, the giant stainless-steel vats stood guard until it was their time to perform.

The Alabamians experienced delays at both JFK and Charles de Gaulle Airports, so our big welcome dinner would also be delayed. Since they would be too jet-lagged and late for a big dinner, I prepared a fresh pot of *ribollita* (Tuscan bread soup), which was ladled into the terracotta bowls and waiting for them when they arrived at 10:00 p.m. This is early for the Italians, and Riccardo and Paola were there to welcome the new guests.

At dinner, Riccardo received permission from *the doctor* to start the harvest. With this news, glasses clinked with a huge *Salute!* Sharing this moment with our hosts was awesome, as was enjoying the *liquid fruits* of their labor!

Within minutes, my guests requested a small change to our itinerary. *Billy T*, a guitar-playin', tractor-drivin' Alabama farm boy, and Alabama Senator *Garlano* (Garlan Gudger) asked if their crew could sleep in a bit the next morning, then spend the remainder of the day working in the vineyard.

Paola and Riccardo couldn't believe their ears and were overcome with gratitude. *A fast friendship was forming.*

THE HARVESTERS

September 28, 2019, was the absolute most glorious day in Tavernelle di Pesa. At 6:00 a.m., the rooster crowed with extra zeal as if to proclaim that harvest had arrived! As I passed Erin's room, I remembered she was going into Firenze with Paola. Although we would miss her on the farm, I knew she would be a great help to Paola at the Mercato and it would be a fun-filled day for her.

Around nine o'clock, *Billy T and Garlano* herded the girls out of the apartment after the Italian caffè and pastries that had been left for them and gathered under my window and shouted, "Good morning, Mama!"

I've known Garlan Gudger since he was in high school and considered him to be like *one of my boys.* His father owned a successful architectural antiques store in Cullman, Alabama. Garlan spent most afternoons and summers working there during high school and college.

He was handsome as a prince *and* one of the hardest-working young men I had ever met, with not an ounce of entitlement within him. I knew he *would make something of himself;* this is *Southern mama* for "he would be successful."

I recall driving to Cullman to pick up an antique door I had purchased for a client. Garlan was home for the summer and carried the door out to load into my Suburban.

As usual, he gave me a big old bear hug and thanked me. I looked way up at him and said, "Garlan Gudger, one of these days, you're going to be the governor of Alabama!"

Well, twenty years later and halfway there, *Alabama Senator Garlan Gudger* and I headed down the road in Tuscany to help my family with their harvest. His servant heart knows no boundaries.

The sky was azure blue, the air crystal clear. Although the sun was hot, the crisp autumn wind cut briskly through each row like a knife.

Until *that* day, I never really understood why my grandmother headed into the field in late August in long sleeves, pants, and a bonnet. I now understand the sun gives a reminder of who is in control, and I do my best to cover what needs protection with sunscreen and a good hat.

When we located Riccardo and farmhands Malik and Modu, they skillfully showed us what to do. With the Tuscan sun on our faces, red buckets at our feet, and green clippers in our hands, we began to experience Italy in a way most people only get to dream about.

As I stood at the top of the vineyard row, capturing photographs of the harvest in action, I thanked God for the most precious moment in time.

My gratitude was not only for the spectacular scene but even more for these amazing people giving up their *vacation time* to help *my famiglia. That* is a picture that surpassed the beautiful Tuscan backdrop in which they all were standing. There are plenty of good Americans still around, *and I was so proud to be spending time in Italy with four of them.*

PARTY IN THE *CUCINA*

The big welcome dinner was rescheduled for *that* evening in *my house,* and there were many things to be done in my *cucina,* so I ran back up the hill and started preparations.

I began, just as Paola and her family have done for centuries, by *peeling tomatoes.* Every morning, I am reminded of these women as I use their kitchen implements.

While rinsing the tomatoes, I heard the *old orange Fiat* returning with a load of grapes just beneath my window. This tractor has also been handed down for several generations— *and it sounded like it!*

I leaned out the window and shouted, "Ciao, Ricca!" He heartily replied, "Ciao Keem-A!" The sound of the tractor and the thick scent of motor oil overwhelmed me as he made his way back down to the vineyard.

I literally sat down in the chair, closed my eyes, and was transported back to Grandmother Lemmons' farm in Missouri. I remembered those exact sounds and smells as Uncle Cleatus pulled into the shed at the end of a long day in the field.

The sense of smell is by far my strongest sense. It usually evokes comfort and sweet memories. It is amazing to me that over fifty years have passed, and I can still remember it so vividly. My happiest days were spent at my grandmother's farm, and this reminder was such a gift.

These new memories are now embedded, perhaps even more as an adult. I am certain one reason I'm so drawn to this place is because of my childhood memories. Life here on this farm is slower, simpler, more intentional...just like those precious care-free days of my youth.

I spent the rest of the day cooking, reminiscing, and preparing for the new events that would occur after the sun went down.

PARTY IN THE *CUCINA*

The celebration started with a sunset toast on the *terrazza*. Riccardo poured his Classico and Riserva Chianti, which was served alongside a sumptuous antipasti platter. The antipasti, however, took a backseat to the incredible sunset, God's signature on a perfect day!

After the last ray disappeared, we headed upstairs to continue the feast. Homemade mushroom ravioli with fresh porcini sauce, followed by roasted chicken infused with heirloom garlic, *insalata mista*, and roasted potatoes with rosemary and sage, all freshly picked from bushes behind my apartment.

Then, on to *dolci* (sweet) Italian bread pudding and the *digestivos*!

While the Italians are *seriously concerned for your health and well-being* and insist that the *digestivos* are solely for digestive purposes, I have come to believe these strong imbibements, in fact, are just more reasons to have a good time! Vin santo, limoncello, grappa, and nocino were slowly sipped while Francesco played Bach's Cello Suite No.1 in G Major. Nothing less would have been appropriate.

The evening culminated with *Billy T* and *Ricca* picking out Johnny Cash tunes on dueling guitars. Then followed dancing to Earth, Wind and Fire's *September*! To quote Frenchy, it was *fantastico!*

As we said goodnight, Riccardo and Paola thanked everyone for their hard work in the vineyard. Five extra sets of hands working gave them a huge head start on the rest of the harvest.

Hugs and kisses were exchanged with new respect. With exhausted bodies and united hearts, the Italians and Americans had moved from *friends to famiglia*.

HARVESTING TUSCANY

Although working in the vineyard was a monumental way start to their trip, all of Tuscany awaited, so we set out bright and early the next day for Firenze, the Birthplace of the Renaissance!

The Uffizi Gallery, Michelangelo's David, and Medici Chapel were the first stops on the list.

After stimulating our minds and filling our tummies, we headed to San Lorenzo Market for a visit with my friend Pasquale Iacovelli. A stop in his fourth-generation leather shop is a must if only to breathe in the rich aroma of Italian leather. I am seriously trying to get him to develop a leather-scented candle!

The last stop of the day was at the Mercato for a *kiss-kiss* from Paola and to peruse all of their goods.

Dinner that night was at *La Fattoria in Tavernelle*, where yet another culinary treat awaited my hungry guests. After two sumptuous courses, *Riccardo Corsini* pulled out all the big guns and arrived with his *bistecca alla fiorentina*, one of the most famous dishes in Tuscan cuisine.

This Italian steak is cut to the bone and cooked on the embers of a huge, open wood fire grill at the entrance of the restaurant. I think I even saw a tear fall from Billy T's eye as Riccardo made his grand entrance with this Flintstone-sized piece of beef! To our surprise, and even after a long day harvesting, *our Riccardo*, Paola, Frenchy, and Erin joined us. Yet another glorious day in Tuscany.

NEXT STOP, FOSDINOVO

No one ever believes me when I tell them about the treacherous road to Fosdinovo. If it wasn't worth the effort, believe me, I would never make the trip. *But it is, and we made the trek.*

After arriving and touring Malaspina Castle, our evening meal was taken just outside the walls at a local *ristorante*, where Fiorella delivered her *sgabei*, which disappeared as soon as they arrived. This cloud-like fried bread is similar to a beignet but savory. It is served alongside a long board of *salumi*, *Lardo di Colonnata*, and *stracchino cheese*. The gooey cheese melts like butter when spooned into this *hot pocket from heaven*.

With full bellies, we trudged back up the hill to the castle. Once we walked thru the fortress walls, we heard church bells and music echoing down the dark alley. Oddly, we also noticed all of the front doors were propped open, and a candle was lit and burning on each stoop.

We followed the music until we came to the piazza, a small common courtyard just outside the Chiesa (church) di San Remigio. The band was leading a long processional of reveling villagers into the church.

The best description of the event would be that we found a good old-fashioned Italian *covered dish dinner*.

Now, if you don't know what that is, a) you are not from the South, and b) *bless your heart!* A *covered dish dinner* is one of the South's most time-honored traditions. It is typically observed after church on a Sunday morning. Of course, it always landed on the hottest day of the year and *immediately* after the last amen. When I was a little girl, it was also called *dinner on the ground*. (This was before we got *too soft* to eat outside with no air-conditioning) Honestly, it was a good move as the cases of food poisoning decreased from eating all the mayonnaise-laced offerings of a good *dinner on the ground*!

This Italian *covered dish* looked like quite a spread. I am certain all the *nonnas* tried to outdo each other with their favorite pasta dishes! There were antipasto platters, breads (with no salt, I'm sure), and the *dolci* (dessert) table!

It was brimming with cannoli, pastries and puddings, fruits and roasted chestnuts, a seasonal delicacy. It was *so* tempting to sneak a bite, but with our stuffed bellies and in respect, we turned our interests to the church and what was going on inside.

On the corner of the church was pinned a poster about the festival activities, which included this *Holy Mass and Eucharistic Adoration service.*

We quietly stood inside the back of the sanctuary and witnessed this time-honored festival that has taken place since the thirteenth century. Surrounded by pearly white Carrara marble altars, a fourteenth-century statue of San Remigio, the Sepulchre of Galetto Malaspina, and a group of reverent congregants, we were immersed in this service that dates back to the 1300s.

The antiquity of this country never ceases to amaze me *and leave me humbled*. At the least, one must stand in awe of the traditions that they have managed to uphold for centuries. As we quietly walked back to the castle through the candlelit street, it wasn't difficult to imagine what it must have been like in 1367. Basically, the only visible differences were the clothes on our backs and the knowledge of the modern day in which we now reside. Nothing else has changed. Not even our modest accommodations.

I reserved the Marchese Malaspina suite for Garlan and Heather. With his vocation, I knew the medieval adornments of this bedroom dating back to the 1100s would be most appreciated. The suite was located in the turret of the original structure, and its authenticity went a step further, with them both hearing a disturbing cry during the night coming from the empty room adjacent to theirs. Thankfully, Lord and Lady Gudger met us unharmed at the breakfast table the next morning.

A KNOCK ON MY DOOR

After two days on the road, it was good to be back *home* on the farm.

Erin shared tales of her adventures since we had been gone, which included a day with Paola at the market and another one in the vineyard helping Riccardo and Frenchy. Her beautiful face had the sun-burned nose to prove it, but the Italian sunshine looked good on her, and I could tell she had fallen in love with my family *and they had fallen in love with her*. Once again, my family expanded.

From the gigantic mound of stems outside the cantina,

which are removed from the picked grapes, I could see that much progress had been made during our absence. We heard that Modu and Malik had not been able to work, which left Riccardo short-handed. Also, rain was predicted for the following day, which was not good. *The remainder of the grapes needed to be harvested immediately.*

The rooster had not even crowed the next morning when I heard a knock at my door.

I threw on my robe, ran down the stairs, and opened the door, only to find *Garlano* standing there with a coffee mug in hand. "Hey, Mama, can we talk?"

Normally, this would be a worrisome scenario, but because it was Garlan, it didn't faze me. In fact, it intrigued and excited me. With that big grin on his face, I could tell he was *up to something*; and he was.

"Hey, Mama, we can't leave them here today with all these grapes to pick by themselves. The rain is coming, and we really want to stay and help. I know you have something really awesome planned for us today, but would you be okay with that?"

Doesn't take a genius to guess the scenario. After shedding a few tears, I poured him another cup of coffee, pulled out a little pancetta, and threw it into a pan.

"Go wake up the gang and come on over in thirty minutes for some breakfast. We will all need a good one before a day of hard work in the vineyard." With a big hug and a wink, he was off.

Without going into detail, that day will *always* be one of my favorite days in Italy.

I *will* tell you, that afternoon, the heavens unleashed, and the rains came, but this hearty group and Erin didn't even flinch. I had gone inside to prepare dinner and expected them to come in once the rain started. They did not. They continued working and returned, drenched to the bone, after the job was finished.

People always ask, "What are some of your favorite moments in Italy?"

This day definitely ranks pretty high. Witnessing these two *countries* working side by side toward a common goal. The harvest needed to be gathered. We did it together.

My group put themselves, their time, their comfort, and their rank aside and *helped someone else while on their vacation*. I am not sure how many guests would have done the same thing if the harvest had occurred during *their* week. I'd like to think all of them would, *and I do*. It has happened every season since.

Although the rest of the trip was filled with pasta-making, gelato-eating, truffle-digging, music-playing, dancing, wine-drinking, and some amazing sights and sounds, *nothing compared to this simple day in Tuscany spent with a man, his farm, and his old orange Fiat.*

MY NEWFOUND FRIEND AND SCULPTOR IN VOLTERRA...
JUST INSIDE THE DOOR.

CHAPTER 10

The Big Black Hat
and White Dust
in the Doorway

*I hope you find, as I did, that happiness comes from
noticing and enjoying the little things in life.*

—BARBARA ANN KIPFER

Founded in the eighth century by the Etruscans, Volterra
is one of the best-preserved and off-the-beaten-path hill
towns in Tuscany.

The fourth-century Porta all'Arco (*The Arch Gate*) is
the only Etruscan wall to have survived World War II. The
Volterrans disassembled it and filled it in, fearing Nazi forces
would destroy the arch in order to slow Allied forces. After
the war's end, it was painstakingly reconstructed, stone by
stone, by the brave citizens of Volterra.

Although the trek down to this historical arch requires some
strong calf muscles, actually, the tough part is walking back *up*
the hill, I do feel it is of great importance as we visit the town.

The most rewarding aspect of travel is learning and making new discoveries. Anthony Bourdain said, "It seems that the more places I see and experience, the bigger I realize the world to be. The more I become aware of, the more I realize how relatively little I know of it, how many places I have still to go, how much more there is to learn."

LEWIS AND CLARK

How Lewis and Clark must have felt as their birchbark canoes cut through the headwaters of the Missouri River, then continued on to the Columbia River, eventually leading them to the Pacific Ocean! Can you imagine all the surprises they found on their expedition?

I am an explorer to the core. Once at a marriage seminar, we were given a test on what kind of dog our personality was most like. Mine was the bloodhound. *Not* a surprise. I also use this fabulous skill set to sniff out bargains at flea markets and even a good TJ Maxx! As my sense of exploration is handy in the shopping sense, moreover, it has also led me into many great adventures along the way.

One of the best stories of *uncharted adventure*s occurred on our honeymoon. We flew into Boston, rented a car, and traveled down the coast. Our first night was spent in Sudbury, Massachusetts, at Longfellow's Wayside Inn, the oldest inn in America. The next morning, we *stumbled upon* the Brimfield Flea Market, the oldest and largest antique market in the country. Vendors line both sides of the highway for miles. We were in heaven!

We continued our trip with stops at Concord, Sturbridge Village, Providence, and a night on Block Island, then finally concluded our honeymoon, spending a few days in Newport, Rhode Island.

For two avid history and antique buffs, Newport was an absolute dream. We stayed at a quaint little inn just across from St. Mary's Catholic Church, where John F. Kennedy and Jacqueline Lee Bouvier were married.

We toured all of the *summer homes*, The Breakers (Vanderbilt), Rosecliff (where The Great Gatsby was filmed), The Marble House, and The Elms, just to name a few.

Our favorite, by far, was *Hammersmith Farm,* a Victorian estate located on Narragansett Bay. It had been the childhood home of First Lady Jacqueline Kennedy *and* the site of the reception for her 1953 wedding to US Senator John F. Kennedy. During his presidency, it was referred to as the *Summer White House.* I knew it well, as I had practically read every book on the planet about Jackie and the Kennedys.

I have always felt uniquely connected to them. Perhaps because I was born on November 27, 1963, the day John F. Kennedy was buried. Or perhaps, like many others, I am drawn to the *triumphant and tragic* story of Camelot. I have an extensive library on the subject, which should have its own card catalog!

As an emerging designer, I was naturally drawn to Jackie, lover of the arts, cuisine, design, fashion, travel, *and the written word.* In fact, I elected to use her as the subject of my college senior portrait study. For our final senior art exhibition, we were assigned to paint a portrait of a famous person. *Who better than Jaqueline Bouvier Kennedy Onassis?* Following the show, I had no plans for the piece, and like many other works from my past, the painting ended up at my parent's home...*my own private gallery*!

As we were touring Hammersmith, I found it odd there were no formal portraits of Jackie in the entire house. Her mother, Janet Auchincloss, sold the house in 1976 to the Newport Historical Society, following the death of her husband. The guide explained the house had remained fully intact: *exactly* as it was since the day of her departure.

We also learned that Mrs. Auchincloss, seventy-eight at the time, was still living on the property in *The Castle* and could occasionally be seen walking the property, especially down by the stables. She, like her daughter, was an excellent equestrienne: a three-time winner of the Hunter Championship at the National Horse Show in New York.

After the tour, I went directly to the docent and began a conversation—one that now astounds me. However, I am proud of that free-spirited and bold young woman who unabashedly offered *my painting* to Hammersmith Farm. Oh, the pride of youth!

Yes, you read that correctly. *I offered my portrait of Jacqueline Kennedy Onassis to the blue-blooded, high-society queens of Newport, Rhode Island!* I still cannot believe it myself. What is even more unbelievable about this story is they seemed thrilled at the thought of receiving it!

My precious daddy. To this day, I do not know how much

it cost him to ship the painting; I never even asked. Fully on board, he immediately shipped it without as much as a whimper. We should note my *bloodhound gene* comes *directly* from my dad, who is always up for a good adventure.

Back to the story.

The agreement was made with *the Society* to deliver the painting on Saturday afternoon, as soon as it arrived via UPS at our bed-and-breakfast in Newport. Thankfully, this was pre-pandemic, and the painting arrived safely *as scheduled*.

Saturday morning, we anxiously drove onto the property. I remember thinking, *What in the world have I done, and what was I thinking? What if they don't like it?*

I also remembered Dad instructing me to attach a small bio card about myself to the back of the painting. When we parked, I quickly jotted down my information on an index card and placed it in between the tightly-stretched canvas and wooden frame. After finishing my bio, I looked up and realized my husband was nowhere to be found. I was intent on being prompt, and it was time to go in. *Where was he?*

About that time, he walked up with a big grin on his face. "Where have you been? We are about to be late for our appointment!"

He smugly replied, "Kim, we are not taking the painting in to them today. Mrs. Auchincloss just invited us to her home this afternoon for tea, a visit, and to see the painting."

What? I replied, "This is *no* time to be joking around!"

He continued by saying that, as we drove onto the property, he noticed an elegantly dressed lady with a huge black hat standing by the fence near the barn. He said that when she extended her hand, the horses immediately ran toward her. I had been too busy writing the bio to notice. He also explained that the reason he even noticed her was due to her resemblance to Jackie. *Who else could it have been?* So, true to form, he walked down to the lady, introduced himself, and informed her of our business.

He was a Southern bee charmer, especially with an older lady. She responded kindly to his introduction and wanted to see the painting. She went on to explain that she was on her way to a wedding in town and wouldn't be available until later in the afternoon. *Could we possibly join her afterward for tea and a visit?*

I nearly passed out with anxiousness, excitement, and nervousness; too many feelings to mention! *But to be showing Jackie's mother the painting? Oh, my goodness!*

While my ex-husband's sense of adventure could be dangerous, it was also one of the attributes that attracted me to him in the first place. We were both bloodhounds, and those traits usually led to exciting times *and* fascinating stories.

With our new agenda, we entered Hammersmith and shared the account with the docent. She was delighted and in full agreement Mrs. Auchincloss should be given the first opportunity of viewing the painting and determining its final destination. We thanked them for their kindness and scurried back to the inn to get ready for tea!

What in the world does one wear when meeting Jacqueline Kennedy's mother for tea?

Oh, how I longed to have packed my winter white *Geiger* jacket and black patent tuxedo pumps! Although I didn't bring those, I did pack *my pearls*, so I slipped them around my neck, pressed my white linen blouse, zipped up my striped skirt, powdered my nose, and out the door we went.

As we approached the car, we noticed a small crowd gathering across the street at St. Mary's Church. Within moments, bride and groom burst through the massive wooden doors and ran through a hail of tossed birdseed, and climbed into the horse-drawn carriage awaiting them. It didn't take long to deduce that *this* was the wedding Mrs. Auchincloss was attending. Standing on the opposite side of the street, with a camera in tow, I shot several pictures of the happy couple as they were whisked away.

On our third anniversary, my husband gave me a copy of the highly-anticipated and celebrated *Martha Stewart Weddings* book. As I thumbed through it, I spotted a familiar scene; a big Newport society wedding with a couple in a horse-drawn carriage in September 1985. Guess who was standing on the other side of the street? The young Nashville honeymooners snapping photos of the bride and groom! Such a surprise and *unexpected* treasure from our honeymoon.

PEARLS AND TEA

Upon arrival to *The Castle,* we were shown into the living room by the butler. He relayed that Mrs. Auchincloss had been delayed and would be joining us as soon as the reception was over. With her regrets for our inconvenience, he offered us tea and biscuits as we waited. I couldn't have been happier to wait. This gave me time to peruse and drink in this surreal moment.

As I perched on the edge of the floral chintz sofa in this most impeccably appointed room, my eyes scanned from corner to corner. What most intrigued me were all the beautifully framed family photographs scattered in groupings on the antique end tables and secretary. These photographs were the very ones I have seen my entire life. However, *these* pictures were not copies; they were *originals*.

Further reality set in but *completely surreal.*

He sat on this sofa; *They* stood in front of this massive pre-Revolutionary stone fireplace on a chilly evening. Pictures of the president and first lady were placed as if they had just left the house. Baby pictures of John John and debutante pictures of Caroline...all sitting around as they do in any grandmother's home.

THE MOTHER

As if awakened from a dream, the front door opened, and Mrs. Auchincloss entered. She removed her large-brimmed black hat and swept into the room like a prima ballerina. Still in high heels at seventy-eight, she was the epitome of elegance and grace, dressed in a tailored silk windowpane plaid dress and pearls. I was an immediate fan. It is no wonder her daughter was such a fashion icon. *Jackie had an impeccable model.*

Mrs. Auchincloss extended her hand and said, "Ah, the young artist." Her eye then caught the portrait, which I had positioned by the stone fireplace, and she replied, "How lovely! Has Jackie seen this?"

Based on her comment, I suspected we might be conversing with an aging mother who might be losing her faculties. Her son Hugh kept close proximity in the adjacent room. I am certain he was wary of this *invasion of young Confederates* whom his mother welcomed into their home and kept a very watchful eye on us.

She invited us to sit while she settled into the dainty chair in front of her twelve-foot mahogany secretary, *which probably came over on the Mayflower*! I replied that Jackie had not seen it and began telling her a bit of my story. As I began, she opened a leather journal and began making notes. She wanted to know where I had studied, who were my instructors, and where we were from. *I am certain she thought us to be more than who we were. We were* not.

After a moment, she pulled her checkbook from the drawer and asked, "How much and to whom do I make out the check?" I gasped! "No, ma'am. This is a gift. It's yours to keep and use as you see fit. There is absolutely no charge. I am beyond honored to be giving it to you."

She stood, glanced over again at the painting with a distant smile, and said, "It is quite lovely. I have always loved this picture and that dress. She had such a pleasant smile in it. Those were happy times."

To hear a mother speak so tenderly about a *happy* time in the life of a daughter who had faced so many tragedies was pure gold. *Those words were the payment.*

The painting was done from one of *my* favorite photographs published on the cover of *Life* magazine in August 1959. The mesmerizing First Lady was dressed in a bubble-gum pink boucle off-the-shoulder dress, with the president gazing at her in the background.

Mrs. Auchincloss finished by jotting down our address. After a bit of small talk, we knew it was time to take our leave, thanked her for her gracious invitation, and were shown to the door.

When we returned from the honeymoon, I shared the story with my painting instructor, Dawn Whitelaw, who was thrilled, nervous, *and* thankful that I hadn't taken any remuneration for the painting as it was a copyright-protected photograph. I'm sure my mother's ingrained saying, "Some things you do for love, not money," was instrumental in this wise decision. I haven't written or thought about this story much since the day it was printed in the *Nashville Tennessean* after we returned home. The framed and faded article still hangs in my office and is a fond memory. It also brings a smile to my face, of *happy times* in *my* life.

Again, I apologize for that lengthy digression from the sunny streets of Italy to this thirty-plus-year-old tale, but it illustrates so well what is yet to come.

WHITE DUST IN VOLTERRA

As we made our way down the steep cobblestone street in Volterra, my guests were peering through the windows of shops that dot this artisan-packed street. There is a guitar maker, a paper store, several sculptors, a wonderful art gallery, and of course, several trattorias.

One of the restaurants was doing a major renovation several years ago and discovered, in the digging, Etruscan ruins under the building. It was fully excavated and now has a glass floor over which patrons may dine.

Like every other narrow street in Italy, it is also adorned with *beautiful doors*. Most are skillfully carved with heavy iron knockers; others, brightly painted and skirted with beautiful flowers, which seem to grow effortlessly even in the shade of the ancient building where they live.

Since my arrival in Tuscany, my imagination runs wild as to what is *behind* those doors. On occasion, I have seen sharply dressed Italian men exiting through the door, hopping on a Vespa, and zooming away. There have been sightings of high-heeled, scarf-clad eighty-five-year-old women slipping out with bags in tow, headed to market.

It is only with greatest fortune that I have now seen *behind* many of these doors. Fortunately, I have spent enough time in Italy to have made Italian acquaintances and garnered invitations to pass *through the door.*

All of this to say, I am constantly looking and investigating *life behind the door...it's that bloodhound gene!*

On this glorious September morning, I followed my guests, snapping photographs of them as they walked down the hill. Nearly at the bottom of the street, I noticed a narrow wooden door that was standing wide open. It wasn't beautiful, nor did it have a sign above or appear to be a shop of any kind.

As I approached, I also noticed a very interesting clue: *a great deal of white dust.* Hmmm. White dust *and* an open door. If my suspicions were correct, I had suspicions of what it could be, and because the door was open, I viewed that as good as a *welcome* mat and went in!

As suspected, I entered a *magical cave* filled with the white wonder for which Volterra is famous: *alabaster.* Stacked from floor to ceiling on wobbly wooden shelves were sculpted vases, animals, icons, plates, everything the mind could possibly imagine. As I slowly turned to my left, I saw a man, seemingly in his late eighties, wedged into a tiny corner by the window. He was completely surrounded by rough, uncut pieces of alabaster stone and was covered from head to toe in white dust. In his hand were a chisel and the intricately crafted vase on which he was carving. As I snapped pictures, he never transferred concentration from his subject.

He spoke not one word of English, but looked up at me, smiled, and said, "*Benvenuta!*" (Welcome!) With broken Italian, I replied, "*Grazie! Lavoro bello! Posso acquistare?*" (Thank you! Beautiful work! May I purchase?) He answered, "*Si!*" with a kind smile and twinkle in his eyes.

"*Un momento,*" (One moment) I said as I scurried up to the hill to locate the Texans and share this treasure trove with them. There are hundreds of shops lining the streets of Volterra, selling exquisite pieces to purchase, but an item coming from the very hands of the humble artist who carved it, to me, was far more valuable an experience than purchasing something in a tourist trap. I also loved knowing that he wouldn't have to share commission.

JUST LOOK UP

This is one of a million illustrations I could share of not missing out on a great opportunity. I could literally write another book simply based on *being at the right place, at the right time. For some reason, it is my gift.* I have learned it typically serves you well to be open to life's spontaneous adventures and be prepared to *seize the day!*

My dear friend and mentor Nelson writes a daily Facebook and Instagram post, which usually ends with "Just look up." Now, I am pretty certain Nelson is not instructing you to literally go outside and look up into the clouds, even though every post is paired with the most thought-provoking images of the earth, sky, and nature.

I believe his intent is to remind us that there is *so* much to be grateful for and experience if we will only open our eyes and receive the daily wonders that God places before us!

Now, thankfully, that day in Volterra, I was looking *down* and saw the white dust, which led me into the doorway of that magical place.

I am *so* glad that on *that* day...I stepped into the adventure. Because of it, my life is so much fuller...just like the day I walked out of the *Little Castle* in Newport, Rhode Island, over thirty years ago.

There are so many *big black hat and white dust* experiences to be found on this incredible journey.

Just look up! For it is in these unexpected moments life's greatest adventures occur!

THE ITALIANS GATHERED IN THE STAIRWELL AFTER DINNER IN MY CASA.

CHAPTER 11

Gioie della Tavola (Joys of the Table)

If the home is the body, the table is the heart, the beating center.

—SHAUNA NIEQUEST

What is the first thing that comes to mind when you hear the word "Italy"?

Perhaps like me, it may be a long table surrounded by a family under a vine-covered pergola on a Tuscan farm. The *mile-long* table is covered with an abundance of home-cooked pastas, meats, cheeses, fruits, and vegetables. The image is complete as each member raises a glass of deep red Chianti to toast *Nonna*, who has prepared this amazing feast.

This scene is one of the most enduring images and metaphors in Italian art, celebrated in the greatest paintings, photography, and films. It also captures what I believe is the core and essence of Italian culture: the joy, warmth, and magic that is the very definition of the Italian table.

Italy is not alone. These traditions are also present in

many other cultures. *Deep bonds of love and friendship are created and strengthened around the dinner table.*

Many years ago, and long before I ever arrived in Italy, I read a fabulous quote written by one of my culinary heroes, Julia Child, which hangs in my kitchen today.

"Dining with one's friends and beloved family is certainly one of life's primal and most innocent delights, one that is both soul-satisfying and eternal."

SUNDAY DINNER

Although I was not born in Italy, this tradition was *not* wasted on me. Some of my very first memories are gathered around a table filled with family, sharing a meal together.

Rarely a Sunday passed when a visiting family or preacher wasn't invited to our home after church for *Sunday dinner*. There was *always* room for more guests around our table, even if it meant there would be less on *our* plates. I am so grateful that this important tradition was rooted deep within me, and I have tried to instill it in my sons.

Many summer evenings were spent squeezing around a table with my thirteen cousins, aunts, and uncles at my Grandmother Lemons' tiny farmhouse on the fertile delta of southern Missouri. As a child, her house didn't seem small at all. It was only after her passing, when I returned to the farm, I actually discovered how small it was. Even more astonishing was how much food came out of that tiny little kitchen.

I'm sure my memory fails me now, and it may have never been as grand a spread as I recall; however, what I do remember *was the magic in those moments.*

Hassel Lemmons wasn't an accomplished chef or even considered to be a *great cook*, but my darling grandmother's *magic* came from the deep love she lavishly poured into her family and the hours of preparation she spent getting ready for us. Just as in the New Testament story of *loaves and fishes,* she *never* ran out of food, room around her table, or the love required to turn those simple meals into something special.

After she died, the only thing I wanted was her *Humpty Dumpty* cookie jar. Every cousin raced to her little kitchen upon entering the house and always found it filled with freshly baked thin and crispy sugar cookies. To be honest, I have never washed the inside of that cookie jar, which now resides in my kitchen. I can still smell *her* in it. That jar still contains the love she had for her family in that little farmhouse in the middle of a soybean field.

Although my recipe may not taste quite the same, it is filled with the same love passed down through three generations to *my* grandbabies.

CINDERELLA'S GLASS SLIPPER

My living quarters shrank drastically following my divorce. Less living space meant smaller kitchens and even smaller dining areas. Entertaining has always been a huge part of my life, and I have all the china, linens, and crystal to prove it. I've always jokingly stated, "Some people do drugs and alcohol...I do china!"

As a designer, I am enamored by a beautifully set table. However, setting one in small spaces can be a challenge and sometimes seems like trying to squeeze my step-sister-sized foot into Cinderella's tiny glass slipper. *Albeit difficult, I will never allow the size or station of my home to be a deterrent to having guests within its walls.*

Famed table and events designer Chantal Larocque said, "There is something about gathering a few favorite people for a meal. A beautifully set table is the perfect canvas for a delicious meal."

Although Chantal's sentiment is correct, and I love a beautifully dressed table, the *canvas* should never be the main objective. The real focus should be who sits in the chairs around it.

Perhaps a better quote came from Cesar Chavez when he penned, "If you want to make a good friend, go to someone's house and eat with him...the people who give you their food, give you their heart."

Some of the greatest joys of my life have been in filling the chairs around my table.

GIOIE DELLA TAVOLA IN ITALIA (JOYS OF THE TABLE IN ITALY)

While on the farm in Tavarnelle, my guests are greeted by Paola, Riccardo, Francesco, and me with a glass of their DOCG-awarded Chianti and a sunset *Salute*!

This is usually at the end of a long travel day, and guests are road-weary, but after settling into their apartment, they are encouraged to join us on the *terrazza* (terrace) to witness their first Tuscan sunset from the farm. It is a jaw-dropping setting, and most are moved to tears at the experience. I honestly cry *every* time, followed by a prayer of thanks for the incredible opportunity I have been given. After the sun has set, then comes the *Festa di Benvenuto*! (Welcome Feast!)

Weather permitting, we dine *al fresco* on the *terrazzo*. However, when the chilly evenings of fall harvest have settled in, we head up the stone stairwell to the *cucina*, or *chicken*, as Paola calls it! *Kitchen and chicken* sound very much alike, and Paola stumbles over the English pronunciation every time! I have now adopted *her version* with a giggle and very fond memories of happy times together.

The *Festa di Benvenuto* typically includes *antipasto* consisting of roasted garlic crostini with fresh ricotta and Paola's fresh basil and red pepper pesto and Crostini Toscana (chicken liver pate...do *not* knock it until you have tried it! It melts in your mouth!); prosciutto and melons, fried sage leaves and hard cheeses. Occasionally, I will share their peach honey drizzled over *coccoli* filled with *stracchino* cheese!

This is followed by the *secondi*; fresh spinach tortellini or *ravioli con funghi* (mushrooms).

Then the *primi*: Riccardo's sizzling grilled chicken or beef with roasted potatoes and eggplant caponata.

Dolci (dessert) consists of chocolate *panna cotta* or white chocolate crème brûlée with fresh berries and biscotti, followed by homemade vinsanto and limoncello from Paola and Riccardo's reserve.

The icing on the cake is Francesco's entertainment as he pulls out his cello and serenades my guests. Times like these shared around the table are what I believe separates typical tours from *living in Italy* with my Italian family and me; being immersed in *gioie della tavola!*

GIOIE DELLA TAVOLA A CASA MIA!

In between guests, if time allows, I explore nearby towns and villages, discovering new restaurants and vendors and making new friends and connections. Most importantly, I try to entertain my Italian friends and family in *casa mia.*

On October 13, 2019, one of the most memorable evenings occurred in my tiny apartment.

Invitations were sent to Paola, Riccardo, and Frenchy; Lorenzo and his girlfriend, Giulia; Loretta Carmagnini and her dashing husband, Luigi; and Emily Woodroof. Despite busy schedules, *all* were able to accept my invitation!

As soon as my American guests departed, I began preparations for the fascinating *cast of character*s who had played such special roles in my first season in Italy. Each of them had helped in very specific ways, and I wanted to thank them in the best way I knew: *by inviting them to join me at* my *table.*

I gathered all the ingredients from Mercato Centrale in Firenze and fresh bread from a local bakery in Tavarnelle.

This meal would not be of Tuscan roots; instead, my Southern heritage would be represented: *country captain chicken, curried rice, steamed broccoli, and an extra-special* contorni *(side)*!

To my astonishment, I found a produce vendor from India at the market in Florence who sells *okra*, so fried okra was added to the menu! Sadly, there were no black-eyed peas in sight. I am definitely going to have to ship those in!

They absolutely loved this Southern delicacy, as did Malik and Modu, two lovely men from Senegal who come every year to help with the grape and olive harvest.

One day during the harvest, I made gumbo and invited them to lunch. With a tear running down his big black cheek, Modu explained this gumbo was very similar to a dish *his* grandmother prepared for him as a young boy in West Africa. Over a cup of soup on a chilly September afternoon, our friendship was bonded. We discussed that many of America's traditional Southern dishes actually came from his homeland. Again, food and sharing it brings continents and traditions together.

SETTING THE SCENE

While supper was cooking, I set the large farm table in my *chicken (kitchen)*, turning it longwise to accommodate the longest extension. I draped it with a lemon-covered blue and yellow Italian linen cloth, purchased from Andrea at one of my favorite linen stores in San Gimignano. Next, I placed Paola's blue and white bone china and an antique silverplate flatware that I had acquired at the antique market in Arezzo.

Multicolored, hand-blown glasses from Venice, an antique set of brass candlesticks, and a purple bouquet of Lisianthus, lavender, and rosemary (all picked from Paola's yard) adorned my simple but elegant table.

As *pièce de resistance*, fairy lights and individually hand-colored place cards from a Venetian paper store were carefully placed at each seat around the table to welcome these special friends.

Peaches were in season, so I decided to make a peach cobbler for dessert. The piecrust was going to be difficult without shortening or a rolling pin. However, I have learned to improvise and used butter for the shortening and an empty wine bottle for the pin!

As I was rolling out the pastry, I imagined Paola's *nonna*, *Annita*, standing in this very kitchen window, watching and waiting for her guests to arrive. What meals did she prepare? Was her heart as anxious as mine for them to arrive? *Si!*

I carefully slid the cobbler into the tiny oven and waited for its glorious aroma to envelope my little casa and my guests as they arrived.

THE GUESTS

The guest list could have literally come from *central casting*.

Riccardo Paolella (nicknamed Ricca). *Good* man. Respected master vintner (winemaker) in the region and owner of the farm. Strong as an ox and dedicated to his craft. Works well into the wee hours in the cantina. *Every single bottle* that leaves his farm is touched by his strong hands. Loves strong caffè *and* grappa. Closet musician who digs Bach, the blues, and Johnny Cash and plays bass guitar like a boss!

Paola Guercini. Piccola (tiny) in stature but with the heart of a lioness. Fifth generation owner of *Agriturismo dell'Annita* and consummate hostess, making every guest feel like family. Chief seller of their products in the Mercato

Centrale in Firenze. Flits up and down that long flight of stairs like a hummingbird, in constant movement. *She owns the heart of her family.*

Francesco Paolella (Frenchy). Crown prince and only son of Paola and Ricca. Works tirelessly on the farm with his Babbo (dad). Handily does the marketing for the farm. Cellist *di amore* who also loves the disco, smelling of fine cologne, my *zuppa*, and beautiful women! Handsome bee charmer who can infiltrate even the coldest of hearts. *To know him is to adore him.*

Lorenzo (Guru) Guiducci. Resident Florentine assistant/ translator who teaches Italian *and* plays bass guitar with a Pink Floyd cover band in Firenze. Doesn't meet a stranger and is quite the savvy tour guide. Infectious laugh and enjoys dining! Lives in the renovated ancient home Michelangelo gave his sister on the outskirts of Firenze. I know, you can't make this stuff up!

Giulia Poli. Lorenzo's partner-in-crime and resident architect whose degree has an emphasis on Antiquity Archaeology. Worked in Castellammare di Stabia, where the Villa San Marco is located (a part of the Archeological Park of *Pompei*, which dates back to the reign of Augustus). Beautiful smile with a bit of mystery, which won the heart of Lore and all who know her.

Emily Woodroof. American Resident Director of Studies at *Lipscomb University* in Florence, Italy. Fell in love with Florence eight years ago and never left. A travel-smith, beautiful, kind, brilliant, and unbelievably talented.

Loretta Angeli. Nonna and chef who teaches private pasta-making classes to university students *and* my Americanos in her home in a suburb of Florence. Greets guests at the door with hair swept up and in two-inch high-heels, looking like a 1950 Italian movie star! Graceful. Beautiful *and* incredibly humble. Makes rolling pasta dough glamorous.

Luigi Carmagnini. Loretta's husband...an *Italian Rock Hudson.* Handsome, quite the fashionista, and kind. *Gigi* is the very definition of a *handsome Italian!* Resident historian and director of a World War II Gothic Line Museum celebrating the history in the region.

And last but not least...Perseo!

Perseo. Luigi and Loretta's white Labrador and faithful four-legged companion. Greeter of the guests and lover of any wayward pasta that might hit the floor.

As each guest arrived, *kiss-kisses* were given with warm hugs. Stories filled the room with laughter. Thankfully Lorenzo and Emily were there for anything that needed translation. However, no translation was necessary for their reaction to my Southern fare—especially the fried okra. They have each now added it to their produce list. What pairs perfectly with a Southern feast? Why, Riccardo's Riserva, of course! Who knew?

Like most Italian dinners, time around the table was utterly suspended.

Every morsel was savored. Every drink, sipped slowly, and each conversation, deep and intentional. There were no cell phone interruptions or guests *stepping out* for other appointments. Each guest appreciated both the meal and our precious time together.

THE SLOW MEAL

Now, at this juncture, I should expound upon the Italian custom of *the slow meal*.

You need not *ever* be in a rush at mealtime in Italy. The *fast meal* simply does *not* exist. I learned this the hard way on my first visit to Italy, trying to squeeze in a quick bite of lunch before a scheduled meeting. Needless to say, my friend was often left standing and waiting for me, I am certain, in an aggravated state.

An Italian's idea of fast food is buying a slice of pizza or cup of gelato on a busy street corner and, afterward, closing their place of business for an hour or two of *reposo* (rest time)! Ah, how I love the way Italians think!

As far as *slow food* goes, I am perfectly suited for this custom, as I am, and always have been, a *slow eater*. I'm a fan!

There was actually a *Slow Food Movement* rooted in the heart of Rome in 1986 when the first McDonald's was set to open near the Spanish Steps. There were protestors carrying bowls of penne pasta and signs reading, "We don't want fast food...we want slow food." Three years after that protest, fifteen countries met in Paris and signed the *Slow Food Manifesto, which rallied against the Fast Life, which disrupts our habits, pervades the privacy of our homes,* and forces us to eat fast food. It went on to say, "We wish to rediscover the flavors and savors of our regional cooking and banish the degrading effects of fast food."[2]

---

2   Heather Dowd, "A Brief History of the Slow Food Movement," Tourissimo, accessed on April 27, 2023, https://www.tourissimo.travel/blog/a-brief-history-of-the-slow-food-movement.

It clearly is not only the food that they are insistent on savoring but also the company. This allows time for meaningful conversation and delightful experiences. Although, at times, *slow food* may be inconvenient, I think it a most wise manifesto, one which we Yanks should keep in mind.

DIGESTIVOS AND DANCING

After the last morsels were eaten, the *digestivos* were brought in. Now, a word about those. These after-dinner drinks are said to aid digestion after a substantial meal. My take is they just prolong the fun and actually stimulate *dancing*; and dance we did!

Of course, in their spare time, the Paolellas attend dance class every week! I was clearly the amateur following their dazzling tango when Frenchy swept his *zia americana* (American aunt) off my feet and attempted to direct me in a tarantella!

After dancing, Francesco once again enchanted us with Bach's Suite No.1. As he soulfully played, I sat quietly, breathing in these final moments, knowing that my *maiden season* in Italy would soon be coming to an end, at least for this season. It was the perfect ending.

This magical *slow evening* culminated by gathering in the ancient stairwell of my apartment for the group photo that is shared at the beginning of this chapter.

Their voices still sweetly echo in that stairwell to this day. Each one, a beloved and cherished *cast member* in my new life. Every second with them, a treasured memory.

I am certain when Julia Child made her famous quote, she must have just spent a good deal of time sitting around an *Italian tavola*. I wonder who sat around *her* table?

WW2 SERGEANT FIRST CLASS WILSON LAWRENCE NICHOLS ENJOYING
A LITTLE R&R WITH A BUDDY IN ITALY IN THE FALL OF 44-SPRING 45.

CHAPTER 12

Remember Who You Are

We all carry, inside us, people who came before us.

—LIAM CALLANAN

One highlight of each trip is an afternoon spent in the home of Loretta and Luigi Carmagnini.

Their apartment is located just off the narrow Scandicci Road leading into Florence. It is the most modern home we will visit and is filled with interesting art, beautiful furnishings, winter-white matching sofas, an herb garden on the terrace, and *Perseo,* their adorable yellow Labrador retriever, who is always ready for a scratch between his ears.

Loretta is a fabulous cook and has taught classes for several universities and study-abroad programs in Florence for years. She put teaching on hold after becoming a *nonna* but thankfully *came out of retirement* for my guests.

The class consists of making homemade pasta. Usually, tortellini with spinach and ricotta filling or tagliatelle (fettuccine) with a simple fresh tomato and butter and sage sauce. She also usually surprises us with a homemade *dolci* (sweet)! When my sister's family arrived, she also treated us to her lasagna. *No* comparison to ours; hers is light and delicate...absolutely heavenly!

The Carmagninis are such gracious hosts, and evenings spent in their home are always special; cooking classes in an Italian home also heightens the experience and makes it even more authentic. The evening culminates gathered around their modern glass table, enjoying the fruits of our labor *together*.

Luigi Carmagnini serves as the director of *Museo Gotica*, which exhibits war material and the history of *the Gothic Line*. Whenever possible, he graciously leads my guests on a private tour of the museum as well as on a hike to *Monte Altuzzi*, where one of the bloodiest battles along the *Gothic Line* occurred. It is a humbling afternoon, one filled with heartache and amazement at the unsurmountable feat accomplished by the young American and Allied soldiers.

I have come to believe this connection between our two countries is very important to everyone's Italian experience, and at each dinner, I encourage Luigi to share stories about the Allied presence in and around Tuscany—especially one in Mugello, involving his family.

Before sharing this story, it is important to give a little history of the Gothic Line. Sadly, I knew very little about it before my time in Italy.

THE LIBERATION OF ITALY

In January 1943, Allied leaders decided to use their massive military resources in the Mediterranean to launch an invasion of Italy, which Prime Minister Winston Churchill called the *soft underbelly of Europe.* "The objectives were to remove Italy from World War II, secure the Mediterranean Sea, and force Germany to divert some divisions from the Russian front and other German divisions from Northern France, where the Allies were planning their cross-Channel landing at Normandy."[3]

When American troops landed on the Italian coast, the German army, which was rapidly taking over the defense of Italy, nearly drove them back into the Tyrrhenian Sea. Germans entrenched in the high Apennine Mountains at Cassino brought the mobile Allied army to a grinding halt for four long months.

The Allied forces became bogged down in driving rains, German air raids, and command hesitation. Where the mountains receded, there were still muddy rolling hills, flooded rivers, and washed-out roads, which hampered the advance and assisted the German defenders. It was brutal terrain, and the conditions were harsh.

THE GOTHIC LINE

In the early summer of 1944, the Allied command in Italy had intended for the next major offensive by the Eighth Army to be launched from Florence through the northern dogleg of the Apennines. This section of mountains formed the anchor point for the last German fortified line in Italy, dubbed the *Gothic Line.*

---

3   Battles in Europe in World War II, "The Italian Campaign," accessed on April 27, 2023, https://canadandww2.weebly.com/italian-campaign.html.

Although Allied forces destroyed many of Italy's historical landmarks and ancient villages, their invasion was viewed as a success because it gave them complete control of the western Mediterranean and paved the way for an invasion of Italy. One month after Italy surrendered to Allied forces, it declared war on Nazi Germany, its onetime Axis powers partner, which *ultimately ended the rule of Benito Mussolini,* the fascist prime minister who had formed an alliance with Nazi Germany in 1936.[4]

STORYTIME WITH LUIGI

In the fall of 2019, my second group was comprised of two eye doctors from Alabama and their wives. I was certain this group would be especially interested in Luigi's work, given that Dr. Nichols' father had been stationed in Italy as a twenty-one-year-old soldier in the Army.

This group began their trip in Rome for a bit of sightseeing, which enabled Dr. Nichols to revisit some of the places where his father had been during the war. One such place was the front steps of the Vatican, where the young soldier shot a photograph just after the Liberation of Rome in 1944. With his father's seventy-five-year-old dog tags, Tim reenacted the moment on those same steps and was transported back to the days of his father's youth.

Now, if there was a poster of a Renaissance man, Dr. Timothy Nichols would be on it. A man of steel and velvet: hunter, fisherman, horticulturist, physician, leather-

---

4   The New York Times, "Oct. 13, 1943 | Italy Switches Sides in World War II," accessed April 27, 2023, https://archive.nytimes.com/learning.blogs.nytimes.com/2011/10/13/oct-13-1943-italy-switches-sides-in-world-war-ii.

craftsman, actor, musician, artist, writer, teacher, speaker, and last but not least, wonderful husband and father.

Seriously, Tim would have studied the stars with da Vinci, dined with the Medicis, carved with Michelangelo and painted the sets for Puccini's latest opera, and played the title role to boot!

I knew Tim, a storyteller himself, and his group would enjoy this riveting story from Luigi, and I asked Gigi to share it that night over dinner.

FEEDING THE TROOPS

In 1944 Luigi's father was a young boy living in the small village of Borgo San Lorenzo when a platoon of weary American soldiers entered, following an intense confrontation with German troops. The Allies had held them at bay but were totally exhausted and hoped to find respite in the nearest village. The soldiers exchanged chewing gum, cigarettes, and their rations in hopes of a good meal and a place to rest for the night. Luigi's family kindly offered them refuge in their barn.

At the break of dawn, the Italians began pooling what little resources they had left in order to prepare a feast for the visiting soldiers. Just as the meal was about to be served, a whistle blew, and an order was made for the troops to return to the line.

The Italians were heartbroken to see their new friends and allies head directly into harm's way. They knew that many of these brave young soldiers would never return to their homeland. Sadly, that evening, many returned to the village, not on foot, but in body bags.

NOT EVEN AN ONION

The next day, as Luigi's *nonna* was preparing dinner, she asked her son (Luigi's father) to go out to the barn and fetch an onion and potato, which were stored in the hayloft. When he climbed up into the loft where the soldiers slept, he discovered *everything* had been eaten.

Although he did not find food, he did find an unfamiliar item and pulled it out for a closer look. It was a shiny gold class ring with three initials carved inside; no doubt, a high school graduation ring or one that had been slipped onto a chain and draped around his neck with a goodbye kiss as he headed off to war.

Luigi's father wore the ring with pride for years to remember those special men who gave their lives for his village and for Italy. He gave the ring to Luigi when he turned twenty-one. He is still visibly shaken as he holds the ring and shares this great story of sacrifice.

As I glanced across the table, Tim was moved to tears. No doubt, he could imagine his young father and comrades as they bedded down in a cold and drafty barn somewhere on a farm in Tuscany. We all cried with him.

These sacrifices made over seventy-five years ago enable all of us the luxury of sitting now around this table together.

Here is a post made by one of my guests after a day spent in the company of Luigi in the fall of 2021.

A poignant Tuscan afternoon spent climbing Monte Altuzzo through the Giogo Pass as we traced the steps of the young American soldiers who would take this formidable 3,035 feet peak during World War II.

It was a key position in the Gothic Line. Germans had spent a year fortifying the area with countless bunkers, block houses, trenches, and fields of barbed wire.

It would take a long week of fierce fighting uphill against the Nazi machine gun placements for the Allied forces to come out on top.

This victory was the initial breach in the Gothic Line and paved the way for continuing the attack northward to the Po Valley.

I felt an enormous sense of guilt that I'd never heard of the Gothic Line, the battle for Monte Altuzzo, and the lives given by so many. Is our selfish and divisive generation worthy of the price paid on so many battlefields? Many of those battlefields and their stories are sadly unknown to us.

—NELSON EDDY

BAD AMERICANS?

Before arriving in Italy, I was concerned about how we would be treated. Our media reminds us daily of how hated Americans are around the world. Why would Italy be any different? We invaded their country and bombed their monuments, castles, and bridges; *why would they like us?*

I beg to differ with our media's assessment. After my first three months in Italy, *I never* experienced anything but kindness, respect, and gratitude for my being there; even when I opened my American mouth and *spoke Southern,* or worse, ordered a cappuccino in the afternoon! They loved me and could not have been more gracious to my clients and me. Now, I might get a sideways smirk when I ask for ice in my water, but even that is now brought with a kiss, especially when dining at *Godipopolo's!*

REMEMBER WHO YOU ARE

As a young girl, my sister and I *never* left the house without hearing our parents say, "Act like somebody and remember who you are." Ever! This old adage still holds true today, no matter where I am...in Italy or any other place in the world.

Anthony Bourdain, one of the greatest travel and food writers, said, "If you take something good with you, hopefully, you leave something good behind."

Many of those brave, young soldiers did just that; *they gave the ultimate gift.*

Others, like Tim's dad and two of my beloved uncles, fought for all of us and the freedoms we enjoy to this date. Many, just out of high school, left the comforts of home, friends, and family to fight in a war on foreign soil so far from home.

Perhaps, as they gave their last hugs to their mom and dad, something similar might have been whispered into their ear: *Remember who you are.*

I pray we can rise above our chaos and division and see beyond selfish ambition. Let's honor the sacrifices our forefathers made on our behalf. *Let's remember who we are.*

FALL HARVEST ON THE FARM IN TAVARNELLE.

CHAPTER 13

The Pruning

*God prunes us when He is about to take us into a
new season of growth and expansion.*

—CHRISTINE CAINE

One late August morning, as I started my run down the
farm road, I was stopped in my tracks by the scene set before
me. The sky was azure blue and was filled with gigantic
clouds, casting amazing shadows on the field. These clouds
were the same kind my oldest son, Joseph, and I would
talk about on a long drive. We would both give our best
description of what we imagined them to be. I love that he
inherited this sense of imagination, and it brought a smile to
my face and a tear to my eye. I stopped, drank it in, and said
a prayer of thanks.

The vines were heavy-laden with deep purple Sangiovese
grapes, almost ready to be harvested. As I walked down a row
to make a few shots, I noticed several vines were full of both
healthy *and* shriveled grapes. *How could this be?*

My Missouri roots from the *Show Me State* were showing, which led me to find the answer.

> Grapevines require yearly pruning in late winter to early spring, removing old wood and making room for the new season's growth. Regular pruning ensures a constant production of healthy, good-quality grapes. As grapevines age, particularly if they haven't been pruned for several years, the ability for new growth reduces, as does the quality of the fruit. In some cases, the grapevine might completely halt fruit production.[5]

Oddly enough, this event occurred on August 31, a very significant day in my life. Clearly, God was sending yet another message for me to think about.

For twenty-nine years, August 31 was my wedding anniversary. This day was typically a happy one, filled with watching our wedding video with the kids and a special dinner celebrating that event in our lives.

However, what once *was* a wonderful day had turned into a painful reminder of failure and loss. I absolutely dreaded seeing it coming and tried to plan around it. On this morning, God gave me such a sweet gift. *A new perspective.*

After making this analogy, I now celebrate this day as the new anniversary of when the Father began cutting the dead parts of my life away so that a new one could begin. This pruning is *not* just in reference to a failed marriage but also in reference to my personal life. This new growth has come in many forms.

---

5 Amelia Allonsy, "How to Bring a Grape Vine Back to Life," SFGATE, accessed April 27, 2023, https://homeguides.sfgate.com/bring-grape-vine-back-life-58925.html.

I have learned total surrender to *His* will for my life and have experienced the emergence of life's greatest blessings. I have found myself in places and situations I never imagined. Through the pain of pruning, I have been given new opportunities to serve Him like never before.

Grazie, Dio, per questo anniversario! Thank you, God, for this anniversary and for continuing to prune me in order to produce *new* and healthy fruit, *even when it hurts!*

ADAPTING

My life's *pruning* has also yielded one of life's greatest lessons: *the art of adapting.*

Adapt (verb): to make fit (as for new use) often by modification; to become adapted.[6]

The art of modification, *learning how to make things fit,* as stated in the very definition, has been a challenge. Sometimes, as hard as I have tried, it seems like the process is unending.

Newsflash. This is *exactly* correct. Adapting is an ongoing, *never-ending process in life.*

Riccardo told me that pruning is the most difficult *and* vital part of vine tending. The cold winter months of January and February are spent doing this backbreaking chore. *Every year.* If it is not done, severe consequences will occur, resulting in poor quality and yield during the harvest.

---

6   Merriam-Webster.com Dictionary, s.v. "adapt," accessed March 5, 2023, https://www.merriam-webster.com/dictionary/adapt.

GLOBAL PRUNING

If we have learned nothing else during the pandemic of 2020, it has been the art of adapting. Could God be pruning us... preparing us for a greater yield? Are we being called to go beyond our wants and rights, *be pruned,* for others?

How many millions of lives have been changed and interrupted during the pandemic? *All of us.* It leveled the playing field. COVID-19 *pruned* all of us. It was uncomfortable, painful, and unwanted.

Weddings, graduations, concerts, and funerals; postponed. Trips, cruises, and vacations planned and saved for over a lifetime; canceled. Churches closed. The list of how our lives have been affected is endless. We were *cut off. Pruned.* Life as we knew it changed.

During the waning days of the pandemic, I was amazed at how China and the Olympic Committee adapted in order to host the 2022 Winter Olympic Games. Costly changes were made, and a new protocol was introduced. For the first time in history, athletes were forced to *go it alone* as parents were unable to attend with them. Training processes were changed. Travel and living conditions were drastically *reinvented* in order for the games to even exist. The 2022 Olympics does not stand alone in the lineup of adaptation.

What made the *Greatest Generation* great? I am convinced learning to adapt during the *Great Depression* taught that generation to be resilient and strong. They were pruned and yielded more than any other generation known to man.

What have we learned? What will *we be called?*

MY DAILY PURSUIT

My favorite Nashville artist and friend, *David Arms*, made an excellent post recently that resonated so deeply with me that I added this chapter just to include it.

With his permission, I share his thoughts below.

> If I've learned anything over the last two years, it is this. One of the greatest tools for living a life with less tension is the ability to adapt. Not adapting in ways that infringe on beliefs or core values, but acknowledging and adapting to less desirable changes that come with life.
>
> Life is full of situations we don't like. Or certainly don't wish for. Loss. Illness. Divisions. Even the consequences of poor choices. The list could go on.
>
> Accepting them doesn't make me like them. It just puts me face to face with reality and requires me to decide what I'll do with them.
>
> Resisting them can be like sandpaper but revealing something less attractive. Irritation. Frustration. Shame. Anger.
>
> Unadaptable is rigid. And rigidness can take a lot of strength and energy to maintain. Its hard shell is often easily broken.
>
> I've learned that adapting is easier. Kinder. Less stressful. Two things I greatly desire. I think it makes for a better life for me and for those around me.
>
> This is my daily pursuit.

ME SINGING ALTO AT MY SHERWOOD KINDERGARTEN
GRADUATION CEREMONY IN ATHENS, TENNESSEE.

CHAPTER 14

Sing Again

He who sings scares away his woes.

—MIGUEL DE CERVANTES

Music has always played a central role in my life.

Both my parents' families were musical and loved to sing. In high school, Mom sang in the glee club and played baritone sax. She traveled with the choristers in college and even sang backup for Pat Boone! Dad played the flute in Chattanooga High's Dynamo Marching Band and loved to sing.

As young parents, they were very intentional in exposing my sister and me to the arts, concerts, plays, and musical events. The first concert I remember attending was conducted by Leonard Bernstein in Knoxville, Tennessee. I was mesmerized by his flying white hair *and* baton, the sound of the orchestra, and of course, getting all dressed up for the event. I still have my autograph book containing his signature...*and* David Cassidy's, but I'll save that tidbit for another story!

As far as *my musical* talent, Mother tells the story about my falling in the bathtub one week before kindergarten graduation. She claimed a bump on the head resulted in my learning how to harmonize. At five years old, I sang "Battle Hymn of the Republic" as a duet with Brett Powers at the Sherwood Forrest Kindergarten graduation of 1968.

My sister and I also took private piano lessons. While I liked it, I was never as successful as she was. Kathryne, ever the rule follower, learned to read music the conventional way, but my impatience surfaced, and rather than reading the notes, I found quicker results playing by ear. Of course, this method did not always produce accuracy, which ultimately led to the demise of any grand piano career aspirations for me!

I recall playing my *Kimberly-Concerto* for piano teacher Marcia Hughes, only to her response, "Hmmm... that was interesting, Kim. Why don't you now play what is on the score?"

My musical/entertaining *career* was well on its way when at six, I landed the starring role of *ringmaster* in my first-grade play. I still have the black waistcoat and pants my mother made for me. I guess I have saved it all these years in the event the Smithsonian calls to obtain it for their permanent collection!

Subsequent roles kept coming; in elementary, middle, and high school; Ruth in *Pirates of Penzance*...Mona Kent in *Dames at Sea*. Actually, that production strengthened my lifelong friendship with director, mentor, and senior English teacher Nelson Eddy. I will mention him later too.

My experience on the stage eventually led to my directorial debut in college in the spring of 1986. *Singarama*, a huge show on the campus of David Lipscomb, was one of the university's premier recruiting events. Our show *Radio, Catch the Wave!* won in every category. I even enlisted my new husband as the music director. Directing this show was one of the most beloved memories of my entire college career. So many leadership lessons and lifelong friendships resulted from that show.

It was no surprise that I would marry someone who also had a passion for music. We met singing in the University's Chorale. You could say it was *love at first song*. Although he was a piano performance major, he could sing like Sinatra, which enamored me even more.

His family also sang and were lovers of music, which was icing on the cake.

The prelude at our wedding lasted over an hour and was comprised of a thirty-voice chorus, a pipe organ, grand piano, harpsichord, string quartet, *and* trumpet. Basically, it was a concert...*and a wedding*.

After college graduation, we moved to his hometown, where he was hired as the minister of music at his home church. Both singing and music continued for the next thirty years, at church *and* in our home with our boys.

In 2006, he was hired by a private Christian school in Huntsville, Alabama, as middle and high school music director. While the musical opportunity was wonderful, the best part was it offered extra time with our sons during their high school years.

Music was a blessed part of our time together as a family and was a constant thread that was never broken. Honestly, from the very start, music was one of the *real* things we shared; *it was a connection that could not be faked.*

NO MORE SONG

Sometime around June 2014, the music stopped. My song was gone. This, not a figurative expression. Absolutely nothing came out. I could not sing a single note. Such a strange feeling, one which I had never experienced.

I began searching for answers, reading books and articles. I even contacted a friend in Nashville who knew a doctor who specialized in vocal disorders.

I discovered muscle tension dysphonia (MTD) is a general term for an imbalance in the coordination of the muscles and breathing patterns needed to create a voice.

Although there are many causes for MTD, such as upper respiratory illnesses or infections, it is also a disorder that can be associated with stress and anxiety. It can manifest and become even more prevalent following trauma or significant stressful life events such as the loss of a loved one or PTSD.

Following the divorce, not only was I experiencing the loss of my voice, but music in general was also a painful reminder of the loss. Each song, especially at church, was connected to a memory *and to my heart.*

I honestly didn't know if or when my voice would *ever* return. While many lyrics were extremely difficult to hear, I did hear the voice of my Father most clearly through the songs and voices of others...so, I listened.

Every night, as I settled into bed, I turned on my playlist and just listened. I realize now a priceless gift during this painful period was learning to be a better listener.

I also learned to be still.

Every day my playlist was specific and would repeat over and over, especially while I slept.

Danny Gokey: "Tell Your Heart to Beat Again"

Stephen Curtis Chapman: "I Will Be Here" and "When Love Takes You In"

Hillary Weeks: "He Hears Me"

Laura Story: "Blessings"

Fernando Ortega: "Give Me Jesus"

Whitney Houston: "I Look to You"

David Phelps: "No More Night"

Andrea Bocelli: "Because We Believe" and "The Prayer"

Last but definitely not least...*Michael W. Smith*.

Michael's music occupied the most real estate on my playlist. His music spoke directly to my heart. "Draw Me Close to You," "The Heart of Worship," "Above All," "Sovereign." His *Worship* album played over and over and over again.

BALM IN GILEAD

During these two *songless years*, Sundays were hard. Sundays are *still* hard.

151

The pew where I spent every Sunday my entire life was now uncomfortable. Sitting there alone was a weekly reminder of the loss. Seeing families and couples leaving for Sunday lunch together was brutal.

In 2016, after a particularly difficult Sunday, I decided to visit a new church. At the time, I honestly needed to go somewhere off the grid where no one knew who I was *or* my story; I longed to be just another face in the crowd.

I previously attended several musical events at a beautiful church only a mile or so from my home. The director of music there was incredibly talented, and the choir, one of the best in the city. On that particular Sunday, I desperately needed to hear some good music and knew I would find it there.

As I slipped quietly into the pew, I heard the introduction of a couple who would be singing the offertory. She sang from a wheelchair, and her husband Peter accompanied her on the piano. Gracie Rosenberger sang one of the most beautiful arrangements of "There is a Balm in Gilead" that I have ever heard, and I have heard many. Although I did not know her, or her me, I connected. *She sang with the conviction that only her circumstances could yield.*

This song and that service were a balm to *my* soul and the first tiny step toward the restoration of my voice...my song.

After church, I searched for the couple on Facebook and discovered we had several mutual friends. I messaged them and thanked them for being such a blessing to my life that day.

It wasn't long until a friendship formed with Peter and Gracie. I started delivering meals to them, as she was experiencing some extreme health difficulties. I discovered that Peter (also a writer) had been Gracie's caregiver for over thirty years after a tragic accident left her a double amputee. *What I also discovered was that helping them helped me.*

Another friendship began to grow with the pastor and his wife, and my new church home was found.

Knowing my love of music, the pastor's wife invited me to join the choir. In my *voice-less* state, I was reluctant but ultimately decided to attend. I had been praying fervently that God would soothe my heart and restore my voice. Hopefully, this would be a step in the right direction.

My first visit was very uncomfortable. The group was tightly-knit but also very loving and welcoming. I basically cried through every practice. Most of the pieces we sang were ones from my past performed with my husband, either in college or over the past thirty years at our church.

Committed, I continued attending practice, and two weeks after joining the choir, a single note emerged.

Although my voice never returned with the strength it once had, I am grateful that even in a weaker state, I can now *sing again.*

JOY BREEDS SONG

Two years later, when I discovered my beloved Italy, *new music* began to fill my heart. Experiencing this country and forming new relationships with its people literally filled my heart with such immense joy.

My new life in Italy helped me trade bitterness and sorrow for love and fulfillment.

THE DAY THE MUSIC STOPPED...*AGAIN*

My 2019 guests in Italy loved Paola, Riccardo, and Frenchy so much that they all chipped in and invited them for their *American debut*! In February 2020, the Italians landed in America and headed due South for a two-week tour of God's country!

From Monelle's fried chicken to Wendell Smith's fried bologna sandwiches to *dog-a-fish and hush-a-poppies* (as Frenchy called it) at the Catfish Cafe in Alabama, we ate our way across the South!

A few days after the Italians' arrival, they began receiving unsettling reports from home about a killer virus that was infiltrating their country at a rapid speed.

Paola, Riccardo, and Frenchy flew out of Nashville *one* week before the complete shutdown of Italy. As we said our teary goodbyes at the Nashville airport, *none* of us expected the magnitude of the tidal wave that was headed our way and that *all* of our lives would soon be changed forever.

Within two weeks, the COVID-19 virus had made its way to our shore, and it soon became clear that this raging storm would not stop until it wreaked havoc around the entire world.

In many ways, just like in *my* life, the *music stopped*.

As the entire world went reeling into the throes of

the pandemic, everything stopped. There were *no* packed stadiums, *no* corporate church services, *no* concerts in the park; the lights even went off on Broadway.

Even in the eerie silence, innovative ways to touch one another through social media and song began to emerge. I remember seeing inspiring videos of Italians singing or playing violins and cellos on their balconies in solidarity and thanksgiving of health care workers.

This may have started in Italy, but it soon caught on around the world.

In America, there were daily videos and posts from Hollywood icons and legendary musicians. Each created their own way to reach out and connect with a world that stood still in the silence.

One such legendary artist was *Michael W. Smith*. He and his wife, Debbie, gathered in their Franklin home every night, read Scripture, sang, and prayed with the world. Each video, a message of hope in desperate times. From my little house in Nashville, like thousands of others, I tuned in. Every night I left encouraged by their message and by Michael's songs.

I also tried to encourage where I could and started a Facebook Live cooking class. My first class was sourdough bread-making...then, each week, a different menu. To my surprise, my audience grew, and at times, a few thousand would join me for the class. Facebook kept me connected, even though I was very alone.

Like the Smiths, I attempted to use *my* gifts to encourage others, which in turn, always lifted my spirits! I also began selling items for pick-up, which I had prepared during the classes.

Although the pandemic was financially difficult, God used that time to provide amazing new opportunities for me.

During the early days of the lockdown in Tennessee, I was asked to prepare meals for the governor and his staff at the capitol. It was such an honor to serve in this capacity. I continued to pray that God would take care of me, and He continued to provide my *daily manna*.

I did not, however, expect the amazing harvest He was preparing for me during this time.

A RIDDLE AND AN IDEA

Now, I am an *idea* girl. Always was...always will be. In fact, now when I tell the Italians *I have an idea*, they stop what they are doing and pull up a chair! It has become quite a joke.

Two weeks before Easter of 2020, a dear friend asked me to assemble riddles written by her father into a book for her special friend. I was happy to assist. When I finished, she offered to pay me. I answered, "Instead of a payment, I have an idea." I am sure she winces when I say these words. She *knows* me!

I explained that Michael W. Smith had *walked thru the fire* with me for several years, and I wanted to gift him and Debbie with a special dinner. No strings or motives...I just wanted to express *my* thanks to them for what they had meant to my life and millions of others across the world in the best way I knew... cooking.

I explained that instead of payment, I would like an introduction. She and the Smiths had a mutual friend, and although reluctant, she understood my intentions and made the request. The very next day, her friend generously made the introduction.

After several phone conversations with Debbie Smith, who was so kind and genuine, I delivered Easter Sunday dinner to them the next week. We met, masked, in their driveway and visited for nearly an hour. Due to the quarantine, theirs were some of the first faces I had seen in person for weeks. Although their table was typically filled with their five children and sixteen grandchildren, this Easter, like me, would be spent alone.

They presented me with a beautiful Easter lily, a signed book, many CDs, and a beautiful hand-written note of thanks. I was overwhelmed by this kind gesture and their interest in my life.

Within the year, *Michael W. and Debbie Smith* were sitting around the table with my amazing family and me... *in Italy. Once again, God's grace and favor leaves me speechless.*

Although my time in Italy with the Smiths was unforgettable, there would be more to this story...*oh, so much more to sing about.*

MICHAEL W. SMITH AND "FRENCHY" MAKING MUSIC IN MY APARTMENT.

CHAPTER 15

Sing Again... Again

I don't sing because I am happy, I am happy because I sing.

—WILLIAM JAMES

After two seasons of canceled Flourish Italy, my heart was literally aching to return, but due to COVID-19 and its continued restrictions, it was not looking very likely, at least until the fall of 2021.

Every week, I Facetimed with Paola, Riccardo, and Frenchy. Never did a call go by without shedding tears and saying a prayer that life as we knew it would return soon. However, the vaccination process was moving much slower in Italy than in America, and times there were still very difficult.

I had hoped to return in the spring of 2021 to work with Paola and Riccardo on a few renovations in their house and cantina, but it appeared like it was going to take an *Act of Congress.*

AN ACT OF CONGRESS

On Thursday, April 15, 2021, I was asked to cater a special birthday dinner for *Papa Don Finto*, his children, the governor and first lady of Tennessee, and Michael W. and Debbie Smith. Don has been a spiritual mentor in the lives of thousands, but especially to these two men. It was a spirit-filled evening filled with praise, prayer, and fellowship.

After dinner, Michael pulled me aside and explained that he had finally received clearance to leave for Italy on May 2 to work on a project with the world's most beloved tenor, Andrea Bocelli, called *The Journey*. Michael and several other world-renowned artists had been invited to join Andrea on a spiritual pilgrimage across Tuscany.

The tour would start in Rome with a blessing from the Pope, then Bocelli would ride his horse down the famous Via Francigenia on horseback, where each guest would ride alongside him. Michael W. Smith was the first to join him in Sutri, where he would perform in an ancient amphitheater with a one-hundred-piece orchestra surrounded by two thousand burning torches. Bocelli's *Journey* would continue with each artist making stops in Montefiascone, Viterbo, and Siena. Ultimately, the grand finale would end at Bocelli's Tuscan farm, *Teatro del Silenzio*, in Lajatico, his hometown. The documentary would share the natural beauty of this amazing country in an attempt to give rebirth to the arts and awaken Italy from its devastating blow during the pandemic.

That evening at the gathering, Michael inquired if I thought it would be possible for him and Debbie to stay at the farm a few days before his work with Bocelli. We also discussed the possibility of my being there to facilitate their time while in Tuscany.

I immediately contacted Paola to see if the space would be available and if travel guests were even allowed at this time. She said that the borders had just opened and they *were* booked. However, French guests had canceled their stay that very day due to a COVID-19 outbreak in their small town. Hurdle number one—averted! The apartment was free!

YOU HAVE TO INSIST

Hurdle number two—Could I get clearance to travel to Italy, especially on such short notice?

I started by reading the latest reports from the CDC and government-issued mandates. Honestly, it looked grim, even by *my* standards, and *most* people would have thrown in the towel! Not me. I was determined, and I began to call any and all connections I could think of. I even contacted the State Department. Against all odds *and* a few naysayers, I forged ahead.

Actually, three things prodded me on.

First, a former employee and friend had just returned from Carrara, Italy, on work-related business, and I got some valuable information on the process that he used.

Secondly, that same *riddle-giver* friend encouraged me to *Go for it!*

Last but not least was something that Michael W. Smith said to me. When I told him about all the obstacles I was

161

facing, he simply said, "Father, let it be so."

That was *all* I needed. I received my *formal work request* from the farm, and four days before my trip, I booked my ticket! I prayed that God would go before me like always and started packing!

Andrea Bocelli actually has a famous quote that I absolutely love. "Destiny has a lot to do with it, but so do *you*! You have to persevere...*You* have to *insist*!"

On the morning I flew out of Nashville, I told my sister, "I *will* meet Andrea Bocelli. Let it be so!" She, knowing me better than probably anyone else in the world, replied, "Sister, I have *no* doubt you will," and gave me her blessing. I am so grateful to my family's encouragement and support along *my* journey. None of them have ever discouraged me from going.

I booked a Delta flight that required three COVID-19 tests before even entering Italy, but it also meant you did not have to quarantine upon arrival. Honestly, I would have endured twenty tests down on my hands and knees.

Upon my arrival to Milano, I held my breath as I handed my work request to the armed Italian Border Patrol. As he sternly stared down the letter, he arrived to the sentence which read, "We hereby send this invitation for work-related matters to Kimberly Whitaker to our headquarters in Tavarnelle as an American chef/assistant for Michael W. Smith (a US entertainer) who is coming to work on a project with Andrea Bocelli." He looked up at me and exclaimed, "Bocelli!"

With a big smile, fanning myself, and batting my

Southern-girl eyelashes, I answered, "*Si!*" With a wink and a smile, he stamped my paper and sent me through. *Grazie Dio!*

ALMOST HOME

As I rode the train from Milano Centrale, my mind was spinning with excitement for the opportunity that awaited me. I was thrilled to see my family again and was anxious to introduce them to Michael and Debbie...and vice versa. I knew that the connection would run deep between them. God was involved, and His plans exceed *all* expectations.

When I arrived at the Santa Maria Novella station in Firenze, Frenchy was waiting with a hug and big tears streaming down his beautiful face. We drove through Firenze with windows down, music blaring, laughing, and smiling all the way!

We drove through the poppy-covered countryside from Florence to Panzano to meet Riccardo and Paola where they set up a booth every Sunday outside the shop and restaurant of famed *Dario Cecchini*. This eighth-generation butcher is one of Italy's most celebrated chefs. His grand personality is only eclipsed by the skill of his knife, which has won him extensive acclaim and many featured roles on the BBC and, most recently, on the Netflix documentary series *Chef's Table*. He is described as a theatrical host, a show-stopper, and an artist. All the above apply.

After eating the best hamburger of my life, Frenchy and I made our way home to the farm, stopping along the side of the road for Frenchy to hop out and pick a bright red poppy for my hair.

When we arrived at the farm, I ascended the staircase and opened the door to my casa, which smelled of the lavender Italian cleaner I adore. It was obvious that Daniela and Paola had *put an extra shine on it* for me. It is impossible to arrive at Annita and *not* feel celebrated in every way.

PREPARING FOR THE SMITHS

I had two days to settle in and prepare for the Smiths' arrival. Fresh *branzino*, vegetables, and flowers were purchased at the Mercato in Firenze, where I first met Paola and Riccardo. I was thrilled to see all the familiar faces, although masked in the market, even though it was noticeably empty. I think seeing *my* face gave them hope that better days were just around the corner. I was heartily welcomed and offered big smiles, some hugs, elbow bumps, and free caffè!

I worried *so* for this country that makes kissing a sport. How could they survive *not* touching? Not *kiss-kissing*? It is at the core of who they are! Air kissing would have to be the new norm, but I was absolutely fine with that. Beyond thankful to be *home*.

THE GOD WINKS BEGIN

On Tuesday morning, I got a text from Michael and Debbie saying they had safely arrived in Rome; then, we received a message from their driver giving us an ETA for arrival to the farm. I prepared a large pot of *zuppa* (soup) for lunch and to tide them over until dinner after resting from the long journey.

At half past three, they arrived in my casa, and the first *God wink* occurred.

A piano resides in my kitchen, which has been in Paola's family for as long as she can remember. They had it tuned for Michael's arrival, which was no easy task *and* expensive; however, they wanted to extend every courtesy to Michael as they knew he would want to practice while staying on the farm.

As I was standing at the stove stirring the soup, Michael W. Smith was playing my piano. Seriously...whose life is this?

The fact that God chose *this* man to be sitting in my kitchen in Italy at the piano still leaves me in awe. If you tracked my *most-listened-to* playlist, it would be *Michael W. Smith*. I have listened to his worship music since my college days in the eighties. Truly a musical legend.

Michael's storied career has spanned over forty years, topping contemporary Christian, gospel, and pop charts. He has been friends with and performed for presidents and was even a very close friend to Reverend Billy Graham, who made a profound impact on his life.

The very first time I met Michael and Debbie, I gave him the most underhanded compliment by saying, "Michael, although you have an amazing voice, that is *not* your greatest gift. Your greatest gift is writing. It is truly inspired and God-breathed."

I do not know of any other artist who has penned more music for the cause of Christ than Michael. His music has been sung and recorded by countless artists across the planet.

Although a music legend, as time passed, I would come to

know that he and Debbie are so much more than the music that has defined their lives.

Sorry, I digressed...let's get back to the story!

As he was playing around on the piano, I asked, "Michael, *what* are you going to perform with Bocelli?"

He turned around to the piano and began to sing.

"This lonely heart will sing again. These barren lungs will breathe again. Through suffering, we're stronger in the palm of His hand. Like a beacon in the night...hope illuminates the sky...reaching for each other...and so we carry on...as the keepers of the light."

After he finished the first phrase, stunned, I turned and stopped him... (I know, who stops Michael W. Smith from singing?) "Michael, what is the title of this song?"

He wheeled around on the stool and said, "Sing Again." I nearly fell out of the kitchen window.

Two weeks before my leaving for Italy; *actually, before I even* knew *I was going to Italy*, I sat down to write my next chapter, titled... "Sing Again."

Yes, the chapter you just read, the recollection of *losing my voice* and how God had faithfully restored it. *However, I did* not *finish it*. My writing was interrupted by a surprise trip to Italy! I felt certain I would have time and the inspiration to finish it while I there.

Well, that inspiration just played it on the piano in my kitchen.

How in the world can *anyone not* believe in the goodness of our heavenly Father? Only God can create moments like these!

MORE TENDER MERCIES

As amazing as this was, God continued to *wow* us with His mercies and provide more supernatural events surrounding this song.

The following morning as we were driving into Firenze, traffic was unusually heavy. Michael was sitting up front with Frenchy when he received the orchestration track of "Sing Again." He immediately downloaded and played it on the stereo system of Frenchy's Alfa Romeo. It was so incredible to be with Michael as *he* heard it for the first time. As the piece began swelling to its grand crescendo, we came to a complete halt in traffic.

Of course, we were sitting in the very middle of the bridge overlooking the Arno, with the Ponte Vecchio in the background! Yet another breathtaking moment!

The final and the most mystical *Sing Again moment* was in Badia a Passignano.

Badia, a beautiful abbey that dates back to 1049, is closed to the public, but I have established a relationship with the order, and I add it to my guests' itinerary whenever possible. This tiny, story-book village is also only ten minutes from the farm, and I knew Michael and Debbie would love it. I was also certain that time spent there could provide a worship-filled moment for all of us.

Paola arranged a private practice for Michael on the organ through Fra Matteo, one of the young abbots, at the end of our day in Firenze so she, Riccardo, Francesco, Carla, and Daniela could join us.

Thankfully, Emily and Lorenzo, my translators and friends from Lipscomb University in Firenze, were also able to fit it into their busy schedules, which is a miracle in itself.

After Michael's organ practice, Fra Matteo took us on an *insider's tour* of the abbey. He shared special places that I had not even seen. Our tour ended in the peaceful and contemplative garden just outside the gigantic wooden doors.

As we were walking back to the chapel, I asked Michael if he would possibly sing a portion of "Sing Again" for the Italians. I knew it would be the most opportune time for him to share it, especially with translators present. I also knew that Michael's voice would absolutely soar in the acoustics of this church. Gracious as ever, Michael agreed.

When we moved into the sanctuary, Lorenzo translated the lyrics, which Michael had specifically written for Italy during the pandemic. He explained that the song was an extra source of pride for him as his son and daughters had collaborated with him on the project.

As we gathered around, Michael began to sing. "This lonely heart will sing again." Then the second line, "These barren lungs will breathe again," and on the third, "Through suffering, we're stronger," the church bell clearly rang one single note. *The exact note he was singing*. Michael turned in amazement.

We all stood there, stunned and in complete awe.

Afterward, Fra Matteo humbly expressed his deep emotion and gratitude to Michael. He also shared that the last year of shutdown had been excruciatingly lonely and difficult, and this had been such a blessing for him. He, like us, was moved by Michael's loving spirit and witness.

THE GATHERING

The evening continued with a sumptuous feast in Casa Paolella as we gathered around the fifteen-foot farm table, which has stood watch in this kitchen for over one hundred years. I purchased placemats because I did not want to hide the deep scars and imperfections of its surface with the usual tablecloth used by Paola. Each mark on that magnificent table stands as a written signature to the legacy of the family and friends who are fortunate enough to sit around it today. Imagine the stories it could tell.

Wine, music, and fellowship were enjoyed as we savored every bite *and* this coveted time together. Michael and Debbie became a part of the family that night and easily understood why this place had become so special to me.

This family lives fully, in the moment, with *all* of their heart. There are fancier villas and wineries in the region, but what *this* place has cannot be purchased or translated into a brochure. The *secret sauce* that makes the magic on this farm is *character and love,* and it is as abundant as the grapes on their vines.

After dinner, we moved to my casa, and the Smiths delivered thoughtful gifts for each family member; signed cello music for Francesco; a harp score for Carla; a Tennessee T-shirt and guitar pick for Riccardo and a beautiful cup towel and scented candle for Paola. Then, a concert from Michael and Francesco.

THE WAY OF THE FATHER

As Michael sat down to the piano, his hands effortlessly moved across the keys. With *front-row seats*, we sat and breathed in the music as he played some of our favorites.

In a moment, he invited Francesco to join him with his cello. They began playing from the score "The Giving." Certainly, accompanying a world-renowned artist is daunting for anyone, especially with music you have never played. Michael sensed Frenchy's frustration and quickly diffused it.

He removed the music and said, "Frenchy, let's do this one...just listen and follow me." He began to play "The Heart of Worship." Francesco's nerves immediately eased; he *listened to the music*, and they played seamlessly together.

This tender moment will always reside in my heart as it reminds me of the Father's love when He senses our frustration.

God gently, *and sometimes* not *so gently*, gives us different paths to follow than the ones we have *written* or planned. He offers *alternate routes* when our ways are hitting the wall.

As a farewell piece, Michael played "Friends are Friends Forever." As Emily translated the song, I held tightly to Paola's tiny hand.

It had been a long day, and we all were fading. Paola and Frenchy would go to the market in Firenze early the next morning, and Michael and Debbie would also leave for their work in Rome, so we gave big Italian hugs and kisses and said our goodbyes.

FRIENDS FOREVER

After everyone was gone, as I was cleaning up remnants of the evening, Francesco slipped in with his cello, sat down, and began playing "The Giving," practicing it over and over, again and again. I glanced over and read the inscription at the bottom of the score. It was signed, "Your Friend Forever, Michael W. Smith."

Michael meant it, and Francesco knew it. Some things, some feelings, need no translation.

That sheet of music is now proudly displayed on a stand in front of their picture which hangs on the stucco walls of Francesco's bedroom.

While I washed dishes, we listened to "Sing Again" as Paola and Riccardo gracefully danced arm-in-arm around the room. Yet another beautiful snapshot I will hold in my heart forever.

When I crawled into my bed, I replayed all the surreal happenings of the past few days, still finding it hard to comprehend.

I thanked my Father for these priceless moments and for placing all of these wonderful people in my path and drifted off to sleep...of course, listening to Michael W. Smith on my iPhone as I had done for so many sleepless nights.

However, this night was different. There were extra stars in the broad Tuscan sky with promises of more amazing adventures to follow.

Early the next morning, there was a knock at my door. Michael dropped in to say goodbye and to personally thank me for their stay. As we were talking, there was a knock at my door.

Without a word, Frenchy entered with his cello. Michael knew and sat down to the piano. Frenchy drew the bow across the strings, and they played "The Giving" one last beautiful time.

I am certain this will not be the last time they play together.

These two are now *Friends Forever.*

NICK BRIGHT AND KRISTIAN KELLY JUST AFTER
"THE PROPOSAL" ON BOCELLI'S FARM IN LAJATICO.

CHAPTER 16

Always Look on the Bright Side

When it rains, look for rainbows.

—OSCAR WILDE

For some reason, I was born an optimist. I have typically always been able to see the positive side of almost any situation. I am not really sure where that came from.

Perhaps it came from my parents, who simply *rolled with the punches* and were pretty quick to figure out a good plan B when plan A fell through.

They were skilled at making a half-empty basket look full. We had very little growing up, but that was news to my sister and me. I never remember wanting for much...maybe with the exception of traveling. However, not many people in our circles traveled much back then, so I really didn't notice. I did long to roam the meadows where Heidi lived and sing with Maria on the snow-capped mountains of Austria where *the hills were alive!*

Mother made most of our clothes, which never bothered

175

me. Actually, I loved that she took us to select the fabrics *and* patterns, which made our clothes even *more special.* Ours were custom-made! I didn't ever know that when she worked all night long making our beautiful little dresses, it was because times were so tight. What I did know, even as a child, was that her work outshone my store-bought clothes. She was an excellent seamstress!

On that note, my talented mother even made my wedding gown. We spent three of the most precious months of my life working together on my *Lady-Diana-look-alike dress*! Although you could fit both of my flower girls in one puff sleeve, it was exactly what I wanted! To me, it was the most beautiful gown that I had ever seen, sewn from the finest white silk taffeta and donned with hundreds of tiny seed pearls and sequins.

My sweet daddy did *all* of the flowers for the wedding, including a five-pound bouquet covered with gardenias and stephanotis. Doing flowers for my wedding was not an easy task. There were thirteen bridesmaids and groomsmen, six children, ushers, and grandparents. I seriously don't know how he did it all. As he was walking me down the aisle, I looked up and noticed that he had formed a *W* with the candelabras in honor of my new name. I truly felt like Lady Diana.

If you haven't guessed already, I think my parents are rock stars! They came from good stock, both from hardworking families of the Great Depression who served their families and others well.

LEMONS INTO LEMONADE

My grandfather (Mom's daddy) died one month after I was born in 1963, and after ten years alone, Grandmother Lemmons and her unmarried sister, Aunt Edna, came to live with us in Nashville. My family lived in a large house that had a full basement apartment, a perfect place for these two little farm ladies to live and be cared for as they grew old together. They spent their golden years quilting, making saltwater taffy and sugar cookies, helping with the family laundry, doing crossword puzzles, and reading the Bible. They also spent it mentoring me.

I fondly remember a day in high school when Grandmother said something to me that made an indelible mark on my life. For some reason, my dad had ruffled my feathers, and I ran downstairs to tattle-tale on him. I am sure whatever he did was probably in response to an ignorant thing I did; I was a teenager with raging hormones!

Anyway, I remember boo-hooing on Grandmother's shoulder, wanting her to join in the pity party, only to have her reply, "But, honey, he has so many good ways."

This was *not* the response I was seeking!

Grandmother Lemmons turned *lemons into lemonade*! She *always* looked for the good in people and found something positive to say. I do not ever remember hearing her say an unkind word about anyone. Well, perhaps besides a negative remark about the *naked-legged girls* on *Hee Haw*!

Subsequently, throughout my life, I have really tried my best to retain this trait, but I guess in *my case*, I have chosen to turn my *lemons into limoncello*!

This attitude brings to mind a happy little tune written in the seventies by Eric Idle. Although I wasn't a huge fan of the movie *The Life of Brian*, I heartily agree with the sentiment Idle shares to look on the bright side of life. It isn't always easy, but it IS there for finding. You MUST look.

CHANGING MY ITINERARY

In May 2021, just as I was beginning to pack for my return flight to the States from Tuscany, I received a phone call from Debbie Smith. After spending a few glorious days with us on the farm, she and Michael W. headed to Rome to begin the *Journey* project with Andrea Bocelli.

It was great to get an update on filming. Debbie shared incredible photos of Michael and Andrea riding horses on the Via Francigena. Michael sat tall in the saddle of his statuesque horse, and Andrea was captured riding his black stallion, who is trained very similarly to a seeing-eye-dog. His command and rapport with this stunning animal are unbelievable.

The more I learn about Andrea Bocelli, the more I am impressed. He is not only an internationally acclaimed tenor and incredibly gifted songwriter, but he is also an incredible human being, as is his beautiful wife, Veronica.

As true Southerners do, we sent a few bottles of wine and olive oil from the farm, along with a business card, with Michael and Debbie to give the Bocellis as a hostess gift.

I was standing next to Riccardo in the kitchen when Veronica Bocelli astonishingly texted him a message of thanks. He walked around for days holding up his phone, grinning, saying, "Veronica Bocelli...in my phone!"

PROJECT PROPOSAL

Debbie quickly changed gears from talking about their time with the Bocellis and turned her attention to another *project* that was brewing.

When Deb shared stories of time on the farm with one of the writers/producers, Kristian Kelly expressed interest in going there after filming was finished. Her boyfriend was planning to join her for the final week of taping; then, they would spend another week exploring the region.

Debbie explained that unbeknownst to Kristian, a proposal was being planned and was to take place at some point during the trip. Debbie knew this was right up my alley and that the farm would be a perfect place for an engagement, especially with *Tinkerbell-me* there to sprinkle on a little pixie dust!

Kristian's friend Andrea Walters, assistant to the producer of the project, was also *in on it* and immediately contacted Nick (the future fiancé). After several *WhatsApp* calls between us, *Project Proposal* was well underway!

Thankfully, accommodations on the farm were available, *and* I was able to reschedule my work at home as well as my return. With *my life* handled, I began making plans for the event and for a meeting with Nick Bright on the farm as soon as he arrived in Italy.

Nick resides in Tulsa, Oklahoma, where he owns a

successful video production company. He and Kristian met while working on a TBN project, and after several years, he was ready now to pop the question!

On Thursday, May 20, 2021, I heard Nick's car pull into the gravel parking lot at Annita. My kitchen window gives me a bird's-eye view of incoming guests below, and I shouted, "Buongiorno, Nick!" Elated to finally meet him in person, I ran down the steps and held out my hand. Instead of a handshake, Nick pulled me in for a big hug and kiss-kiss. I felt as if one of *my boys* had arrived!

What a doll. With jet-black hair, a Hollywood smile, and accompanying dimples, it was most obvious how Kristian's heart had been completely captured. I was smitten as well and felt honored to be helping him plan this very important event.

After a quick tour and an introduction to Frenchy and Riccardo, we gathered on the terrace where the proposal would take place. This is undoubtedly one of the most stunning views in the area, a picture-perfect setting in which to propose. I shared my thoughts about the meal I would prepare for them; candles, flowers, and of course, the wonderful addition of Francesco, who offered to play his cello in the background.

The plan was for Nick and Kris to arrive Monday afternoon following the final day of taping on Sunday at Bocelli's farm in Lajatico. Around sunset, they would join me for dinner on the terrace. At that point, Nick and *the question* would be center stage *under the Tuscan sun* as the spotlight!

Over a glass of Riccardo's prize-winning Chianti, I

listened as Nick explained why he wished to spend the rest of his life with Kristian. I was immediately invested and would pull out all the stops to make sure this event was perfect in every way.

My plan was a perfect one, *except...*

According to the latest weather forecast, there was a 95 percent chance of rain for Monday. Those odds sounded pretty convincing, even for my math-challenged mind. Monday was going to be a complete rain-out.

I verified this with local *staff meteorologist* Riccardo Paolella who could be a professional weatherman after farming for over thirty years. He knows all the signs and trends, and it sounded like the rain was imminent.

After much discussion about alternate ideas on the farm for a rainy-day proposal, *I had another idea.* Enter *plan B.*

THE BRIGHT SIDE (PLAN B)

The weather forecast predicted *Sunday* to be absolutely beautiful: Mid-sixties, sunny and warm, with mild winds and absolutely *no* rain.

Hmmm...I knew that the last day of filming was to be on the Bocelli farm...

Hmmm... Beautiful day...Hmmm...

Those of you who know me know exactly what is coming!

Why not ask if the proposal could take place Sunday on the Bocelli farm?

Nick sat for a second, pondering the suggestion. Then replied, "Kim, I can't interrupt this major production *and* just ask Andrea Bocelli for permission to bust up the joint for my proposal!"

I looked at him and said, "*Why* on earth *not*?! Nick, Kristian has been working side-by-side with Bocelli and this crew every day for over a month. I feel pretty certain that everyone would be on board!"

I further contended that we could run it by production assistant *Andrea Walters*. I knew she would be key. The worst thing that could happen would be if Tom Newman, the producer, said no. If he did, then we would go to plan C. Nor harm, no foul.

At that moment, I felt more like Nick's coach than his proposal director. I felt like I was sending him in for the final play of the game!

With a hug and kiss, I sent him off with a plan *and* on my knees that he would run this play directly into the endzone.

One of my favorite inspirational speakers, Simon Sinek, wrote, "Always plan for the fact that no plan ever goes according to plan."

Lord, please help this plan work!

HERE SHE IS MISS AMERICA

We interrupt this program to bring you a very important message.

Please forgive this *huge* deviation from the story, but

the aforementioned plan B moment reminded me of an illustration that occurred during my tenure at Haul Couture when our perfect plans fell apart, and I was left looking for an alternate play in the fourth quarter!

Please stay with me. I promise not to leave Nick hanging!

Now, for this story, pack your suitcase. We're gonna travel back in time to the bright lights of Neon City.

LAS VEGAS, NEVADA, JANUARY 2011

The marketing strategy at my company, Haul Couture, began by attending Junior League and other juried trade shows across the Southeast. In January 2011, one of my employees got wind of a show lead from his friend and former *Miss New York, Jackie Holmes*. She reported that the Miss America Pageant, which was held in Las Vegas, also had a trade show which ran concurrently with the pageant. Vendors from all over the country rented space in the convention center and sold products to the contestants *and* their *huge* following of family, fans, and friends.

This show was predicted to be a banner year, as it was celebrating the show's seventy-fifth anniversary. We knew Haul Couture was perfect for these women as they schlepped everything from sashes and stilettos to crinolines and crowns!

We applied and were immediately accepted. With less than two weeks to prepare, we frantically began bundling Cargo bags, boards, props, and signs on two pallets and shipped them directly to the convention site, praying they would arrive on time. Not to be outshone by the bags, we packed our snazziest show duds and headed to Vegas!

There are fewer men in the world I love more than William Lamar Casey. He makes me laugh to the core and will always be one of my all-time favorite partners in crime. I love his folks and consider him another one of *my boys*. I have loved every crazy moment we have ever shared.

After checking in to the hotel, we made our traditional buying trip to *the Teej (TJ Maxx)*, set up the bags, and put the final touches on a fabulous booth.

When the doors to the convention center opened, we witnessed a parade of *every animal on the ark*. This show is as diverse as the fifty states it represents. However, even with as many attendees as were present, we didn't seem to be attracting the following we anticipated, nor were we selling bags. Haul Couture was *not* the star we normally were, and our feelings were hurt.

TAKING IT TO THE STREETS

Day two, and still *nothing...except the Shoe Parade*. During the pageant, every contestant was required to represent their state in the annual Shoe Parade. Over ten thousand people would line the parade route to cheer on their girl, so I made an executive decision. We would close the booth during the parade, especially since we knew only *crickets* would be in the exhibit hall during this event. We would take Haul Couture to the streets!

Company rules stated that none of us were ever to walk around a show without a Haul Couture bag. Even a trip to the bathroom *required* it. I made more deals standing in lines for the bathroom and lunch than I can count on one hand.

This show would be no exception. We donned *our* best shoes, grabbed a bag, and headed for the red carpet in hopes of drumming up some business.

While watching each girl sashay around the circle, waving with their state-decorated shoe, I noticed a fancy motorcoach with tinted windows arrive and park right next to the parade route.

Now, being from Nashville, I have learned to keep an eye on these types of busses. They typically produce interesting passengers. While everyone else was occupied watching the parade, I inched over for a closer look at this bus *and* its contents.

When the doors opened, a group of beautifully coiffed, dressed, and poised women gracefully stepped off of the bus. Upon closer attention, I recognized the first beautiful face; actress and Miss America 1955, Lee Meriwether. Following Lee was Phyllis George, 1971; then Gretchen Carlson, 1988 and Heather Whitestone, 1995; the group continued to file off the bus and directly into the parade line-up. *The Formers* had arrived!

I really had to contain my emotions as seeing these women brought back such fond memories of *Miss America Night* when I was a little girl. It was one of the most anticipated nights of the year at our house. Dad would disappear while my mom, sister, and I were glued to the pageant on our television set. Eating an *Old El Paso Mexican*

TV Dinner in the den was also a *huge* treat *and* part of the tradition. All three of us anxiously awaited the talent competition, then the crowning of Miss America! My modest mama usually made us take a bathroom break during the swimsuit competition, as there were no controls to fast-forward through this risqué part of the show!

Every little girl in America wanted to be just like these women, and forty years later, I was standing here in a puddle next to *all* of them!

Although my eyes may have been filled with tears, my business wheels began turning, and I concocted an incredible idea.

While the ladies were making *their* final turn about the plaza, I slipped over and had a conversation with the bus driver. With all the *pageant-girl and world-peace moxie* I could muster, I asked if it would be possible for me to speak to the ladies once they returned to the bus. I don't remember exactly what I said to him, but whatever it was did the job. I'm betting there may have been a bag in it for his wife or a yummy bite to eat.

Once the ladies returned to the bus, I climbed aboard. It was time for my *talent competition* to begin! If only I had brought my baton!

With a Cargo bag on my arm, I conveyed my gratitude for making such a positive impression in my life and in the lives of millions of other little girls. *Fact*: Miss America is more than a beauty contest, a crown, or a title. This program encourages young women to dream big, have their voices heard, and inspire change in the world around them. Each of these successful women had spent a great deal of their lives doing just that.

Following my *sappy but sincere soliloquy*, I invited them to stop by our booth and pick up a Haul Couture Cargo Bag as a gift, each specially pinned with a rhinestone crown.

Within thirty minutes, these women and their throng of pageant groupies flooded into *Haul Couture Vegas*, and our show stats skyrocketed! One would have thought that *Elvis was in the building!*

The most exciting turn of events occurred when Mary Haskell stopped by. Mary, a former Miss Mississippi, bought a few bags *and* introduced us to her husband, Sam, the CEO of Miss America. They graciously surprised us with fifth-row tickets to the show *and* offered to present the newly crowned 2011 Miss America with a Haul Couture Cargo bag!

Incredibly, this strategic marketing move ultimately led to Haul Couture's being selected as one of Hoda and Kathie Lee Gifford's Favorite Things on NBC's *Today Show*.

Our new friend, Sam Haskell, also an Emmy-nominated producer, actually discovered Kathie Lee Gifford during his tenure as Head of Television at the William Morris Agency. Sam and Mary were still close friends with her and presented a bag to Kathie Lee when they accompanied Teresa Scanlin, *Miss America* 2011, to New York for her national interview tour immediately following the pageant.

The trajectory that this seized opportunity made was long-lasting for the company.

Moral of the story...Keep your eyes open. Watch for opportunities and be ready to *act*, especially during challenging or disappointing times. These dead ends or detours are typically God's way of maneuvering magical moments!

OKAY...MEANWHILE, BACK AT THE RANCH IN TAVARNELLE

Saturday night was getting late, and there was still no word from *fiancé-to-be* Nick Bright. Finally, at 11:00 p.m., my phone rang. It was Nick, and he uttered two words... *It's on!*

He continued by saying the director had given a resounding *yes! and* that the Bocellis were overjoyed to add this extra *finale* for Kristian.

Nick added, "But, Ms. Kim, there is *one* thing. I can't do this without your help. Can you please come? And can you bring Francesco with you?"

Hold the phone! Did I just hear what I thought I heard? *An invitation to Andrea Bocelli's farm?*

I glanced over and saw Frenchy on his hands and knees, with tears welling up in his eyes.

You have to understand; in Italy, Andrea Bocelli is second only to the Pope...and he is much less controversial! Andrea is one of, if not *the* biggest celebrity in the entire country, and to Francesco, a cellist and musician, this was almost too much to take in.

It was for me too.

In an earlier chapter, I conveyed the significance of *Michael W. Smith's* music to me. In many ways, it has been the *soundtrack of my life*. Also on that soundtrack would be the music of *Andrea Bocelli*.

Please understand *this is* not *a fan crush*. I've been around big names and celebrities my entire life. For some strange reason, they seem to pop up everywhere I go, and I have had interaction with many of them. No autographs or photos, just interesting conversations.

These *interactions* were not just backstage at a concert or while walking down the streets of New York. *For* some *reason,* God specifically and uniquely wove *these specific people* into the tapestry of my life. Their part in *my story* was written by the greatest composer of all time, my heavenly Father.

My thankfulness and gratitude simply cannot be conveyed.

A SUNDAY DRIVE

I have been on many Sunday drives in my life, but this one was different. This morning, Frenchy and I dressed in our Sunday best, gathered the flowers I had arranged for Kristian, and headed to Lajatico.

As Francesco skillfully whizzed around the mountain curves, anticipation was building. I do not know when I have ever been more excited about an invitation. This one was a *double feature*! Being present at the finale taping of Bocelli's Journey *and* sharing in this life-defining moment for Nick and Kristian was an incredible joy and privilege!

At 9:00 a.m. (2:00 a.m. Nashville time), my sister Kathryne groggily answered the phone. "Hello?"

I nonchalantly replied, "Good morning, sis. Just wanted to give you a quick call to let you know that Frenchy and I are on our way to Andrea Bocelli's farm."

What? She giggled and said, "Exactly as I had predicted! Of course, you are, little sister... only you!"

My parents and the *riddle-giver's* response was very similar. They each wished us luck and said a blessing over our day.

At 10:00 a.m., we pulled up to base camp where the security detail that surrounded *Teatro del Silenzio* was stationed. We rolled down the window and gave them our information.

Our names were on the list, and we headed to the set.

That rainy Monday forecast turned this day into a very *bright* one, especially for Nick and his bride-to-be!

I'll never sing "Always look on the bright side of life" quite the same way again.

Now, I sing it with a grin and a memory of how the Father orchestrated the moment when a *bright* boy got down on one knee on a heavenly farm in Tuscany.

TEATRO DEL SILENZO; FINAL SITE
OF ANDREA BOCELLI'S THE JOURNEY FILM.

CHAPTER 17

The Journey

We must be willing to let go of the life we have planned, so as to have the life that is waiting for us.

—E. M. FORSTER

As Francesco and I drove onto the property at Teatro del Silenzio, our hearts were racing in anticipation of the events that would soon ensue. First, we were instructed to go to the medical pavilion for COVID-19 testing. Even though I knew this was a required procedure, the thought never even occurred to me that a positive test could prevent us from entering. Thankfully, we both were cleared to enter, and we made our way down the hill to the filming site.

Although I had seen photographs of the amphitheater, none of them prepared me for what we saw. Nestled on a hillside in Lajatico, this hidden jewel provides a 180-degree view of the most splendid countryside I have ever seen. Amazingly, this outdoor theatre has not disrupted its natural environment but instead has enhanced it.

In 2005, Andrea Bocelli convinced the local governing

body of Lajatico, where he was born in 1958, to build an outdoor venue whose structure would utilize the natural formations of the hilly landscapes that surround it. This natural *stage* is surrounded by a formation of giant travertine blocks, symbolizing an ancient place of worship.

A pond once used by farmers to water livestock is the present location, and in the center of it resides a glorious sculpture. Every year, a contemporary artist is commissioned to create a monumental piece based on the theme of that year's program. This particular sculpture was a giant golden-bronze tree.

Every July, the theater opens for two days and hosts a concert that welcomes international artists of song, music, and dance who perform with Andrea at this place he calls *home*.

The first production there occurred in July 2006 when Bocelli dedicated the concert to his beloved father.

Guest artists have included Placido Domingo, Jose Carreras, Chris Botti, Kenny G, Heather Headley, Katherine Jenkins, the Orchestra del Maggio Musicale Fiorentino, Gina Lollobrigida, 2Cellos, Stephan Hauser, and famed conductor Zubin Mehta.

After each event concludes, that night, *everything* is removed, and the Teatro del Silenzio returns to being a place of silence and meditation for the other 363 days a year. Thankfully, 2020 was an exception to this rule, and the concluding segment of *The Journey* was filmed here.

As we made our way down the hill, we witnessed the crew setting up the scaffolding and booms for the shoot. I couldn't help but get teary-eyed about the *other production* also underway for Nick and Kristian.

Let me just say I could have won *Best Supporting Actress* upon meeting the fiancée-to-be.

When Andrea Walters introduced me to Kristian Kelly as the *Smiths' friend*, I poured on the innocent charm of a stand-by guest who had been invited to the taping because of my relationship with Michel W. and Debbie Smith. We chitchatted for a moment about them and about the farm she so desperately wanted to visit. After she was called away for script reviews, I had the opportunity to sit and visit with Tom Newman, the producer, who was thrilled about this impending surprise for his friend and colleague, Kris. I enlisted Tom's adorable granddaughter, Daisy, to present flowers to Kristian after the proposal. She had traveled to Italy with her mother to experience the taping on her grandfather's set and was perfect for the *role*!

I won my second Oscar for *supporting actress* when Kristian introduced me to Nick. I pretended as if we had never met while we exchanged grins and as he inconspicuously slipped his cell phone into my pocket for me to record the engagement.

Quietly, a white Range Rover pulled up to the tent. The Bocellis stepped out. Andrea, taller and even more handsome than I had seen in photographs, emerged dressed in a crisp white linen shirt and black pants. Veronica's natural beauty was only equaled by the splendid landscape that surrounded us; absolutely stunning. As I watched her walk with him, the phrase "Behind every successful man, there is a strong woman" immediately came to mind. Her devotion to Andrea was clearly displayed. Their children and two dogs also emerged from the car. Not only are they one of the most beautiful families I have ever seen, but they also seemed to be kind and genuine.

I noticed Andrea's mother was also there. After meeting Andrea and Veronica, I stooped down and said, "*Grazie per aver dato al mondo questo figlio dotato*" (Thank you for giving the world this gifted son).

She held out her hand and graciously accepted my compliment, nodding, "*Grazie a Dio, non a me*" (Thank You, God; not me). Clearly, this great man came from a great mother, one who had been advised to abort him because he would be born with a disability. Thankfully, she did not and bore a child with the voice of an angel.

READY, SET, ACTION

Finally, the hour had arrived for the taping to begin. Katherine Jenkins, acclaimed UK soprano, stepped up elegantly dressed in a gossamer white gown and began to sing with the 120-piece orchestra, which had gathered around the golden tree.

After her solo piece, Andrea joined her to sing "I Believe." Their voices are distinctly suited for each other, and this collaboration could not have been a more perfect prelude to this moment.

I perched in between Francesco and Veronica Bocelli under the scaffolding with our phones, anxiously ready to go *live* on Facebook and Instagram. Hundreds of friends and family from around the world sent well-wishes, hearts, and likes as Nick lowered to a knee and asked for her hand. A breeze swept over them and across this glorious landscape, setting the perfect stage for this God-breathed occasion.

Nick's carefully selected words, "Kristian, there is no one else in this world with whom I'd rather share this Journey," were the perfect finale to this incredible project.

My small role in this *production* was a success, but there was more to come.

LIFE'S UPS AND DOWNS

Although the *Journey* project was a wrap, Kristian and Nick's *journey* was just beginning, starting with a visit to the farm in Tavarnelle. We spent several days celebrating with them and basking in their light which brightly shone as they entered a room.

One of the best offerings at *Flourish Tuscany* is definitely the hot air balloon excursion. If you do nothing else, *this is a must*. Even those who have pushed back due to fear of heights have said it is the highlight of their trip and not one to miss.

I was thrilled that Nick and Kris wanted to add it to their stay, and on their second day, they joined Carla, Francesco, and me at 6:00 a.m. Although our late-night dinner the night before made it really difficult to drag ourselves out of bed so early, it was necessary for the safest flying conditions.

Massimiliano (Max) Catalani, who has piloted over Tuscany for nearly thirty years, welcomed everyone into the balloon as we prepared for takeoff. Although he is always cordial, he takes this responsibility very seriously and commands everyone's complete attention as he gives specific instructions for the flight.

On that particular morning, there was no sunshine peeking over the mountains to help us wake up. Even though the weather forecast had predicted a nice day, the fog was overhead. I sensed Max's concern as we entered the basket.

Just as we reached the typical altitude in which to take flight, he looked over at me with a very serious look in his eyes and said, "No, Kim...this is not good. We must go down." With no further conversation, he lowered the basket and landed it in the same field. Although the scrub was disappointing, I knew we could reschedule. He shared that he could have maneuvered the fog but did not feel good about it and landed. In his opinion, the risk was too great. Bravado may have encouraged another pilot to continue, but I am thankful that Max's wisdom and experience override his ego.

We returned to the farm after rescheduling, and within the hour, Nick and Kris arrived in my kitchen. I prepared a much-needed Americano breakfast, and a precious conversation ensued. In fact, a conversation that would lead to the publication of this book. Again, God moves in mysterious ways!

This scrubbed flight won't be the last diversion these two will face on their *journey* together. It is obvious that they have learned how to maneuver life's ups and downs together. No doubt, they are a strong team, and I cannot wait to see what they will accomplish together.

On their final night at the farm, sitting around Paola and Riccardo's table were five couples, all in different stages of their lives, each with a love story of their own...each a *journey* with peaks and valleys, each an ending yet to be written.

Thankfully, I will never lose faith in true love. Although my *journey* did not have the ending I anticipated, I am encouraged to see beautiful ones in the lives God has placed around me. Their journeys gird my faith that true love *still exists*.

I also live in faith and anticipation that *my journey has yet to be revealed.*

FRIEND AND ARTIST, ANTONIO FRANCESCHETTI AND
HIS LOVELY WIFE STEFANIA IN HIS TAVARNELLE GALLERY.

CHAPTER 18

The Survivors

Every time I witness a strong person, I want to know: what darkness did you conquer in your story? Mountains do not rise without earthquakes.

—KATHERINE MACKENETT

Spring of 2022 was bursting with color and new adventures! I couldn't wait to return to Tuscany with a full schedule of clients. Life was re-emerging after two dreadful years of the pandemic in Italy *and* in America. People were ready to travel, even if it meant still masking up and taking those annoying COVID-19 tests.

I suspected my spring guests were going to be adventurers... and they were.

My first guests were a family affair; a business acquaintance and his beautiful wife, his mother, and his sister. We had to strap on our skates to keep up with *MawMaw*. This seventy-eight-year-old wasn't going to miss a beat, and she didn't. She trudged up and down every cobblestone street, tasted every local dish, rolled pasta like a pro, and climbed up into the hot-air balloon like a teenager! She savored every moment of what Tuscany had to offer. Her sweet attitude was contagious to the Italians and us. She was proof that you are never too old to enjoy the wonders of this amazing country.

On their last night, as we were dining with the Paolellas, *Alano* appropriately named Paola's *coccoli* fried pillows. *Coccoli*, literally translated as "cuddles" in English, are small balls of dough fried in olive oil and are traditionally stuffed with prosciutto and a creamy cheese called *stracchino*. Heavenly!

After *goodbye cuddles* were made with group one, they were off. It is always so hard saying goodbye to my clients, but like many others, I knew they would return.

Following their departure, I built a small break for a bit of work: writing and shopping.

After finding so many amazing antique markets in Italy, I spoke to several friends at home with stores and the possibility of me buying antiques for them and shipping them back. A few jumped in, and a plan was made.

Although I had been to Lucca many times, I had never been there during the antique market and was anxious to see what it offered. One thing I did know was the flat alleys of Lucca would be much easier to maneuver than the steep cobblestones of Arezzo. I made a reservation at a new hotel and decided to phone a friend!

TIME IN ITALY IS *ALWAYS* BEST WHEN SHARED

Several months before my spring arrival, I received a message from a fellow *americana* who lives in Texas. We had a mutual friend who knew about my Italian escapades and shared my contact information. Shelley reached out to see if I might have any recommendations of an Italian realtor or if I knew of any available properties in the area. A friend of hers was looking to purchase a villa just outside of Florence, and Shelley would be helping her with the renovation. In no time, a perfect villa was found, and Shelley arrived to help begin the process.

I could tell from our conversations she was *my kind of girl*, and I couldn't wait to meet her.

One of the things I love about meeting new friends in Italy (especially Americans) is these people seem to possess the same sense of adventure as me, and we are typically a great match!

Although we had never met in person, I invited Shelley to join me in Lucca. Fortunately, she was up for an adventure and accepted my offer. We arrived in Lucca too late to shop, but we had worked up an appetite.

We checked in and headed to Pistoia, which was only minutes away, for dinner at La Taverna dei Miracoli da Mangiafuoco, one of my favorite *ristorantes* in all of Italy! As usual, our meal was absolute perfection. After fulling our tummies with delicacies from the nimble hands of Chef Sonia and big bear hugs from Massimo, we were ready to snuggle in for a good night's rest before our shopping adventure in Lucca.

Like thoroughbred horses, we shot out of the gates early the following morning with market baskets in tow! Lucca was an absolute *wonderland*. Each piazza was brimming with one-of-a-kind treasures. Every narrow cobblestone street was lined with antiques, many dating back to before *our* country was even born!

Rain was predicted, but that did not dampen our excitement. Around lunch, clouds rolled in, and it began to sprinkle. *Smart locals* ran for the nearest caffè or awning to escape this sudden downburst, *but we carried on* in hopes of finding extra treasures without so many shoppers. As fate, *or the Father*, would have it, just as I spotted some fabulous linens, the bottom fell out. The proprietor of the booth kindly invited us to shelter under her tent until the rain passed, and we gladly accepted.

To my surprise, she spoke perfect English and was as kind as she was pretty! Her collection, exquisite; snow-white and impeccably pressed embroidered linens, hand-blown Murano glass chandeliers and fixtures, Italian cut crystal, leather-bound books, fine art, and silver.

Within moments, I had collected a hefty stack of treasures. What I didn't realize was that I had also just discovered a treasured new friend, *Stefania Zocchi*.

IT'S A SMALL WORLD AFTER ALL

Stefania asked the proverbial Italian question, "What are you doing here?" My typical response, in Italian, is, "*Vivo tre mesi in primavera e tre mesi in autunno a Tavarnelle Val di Pesa*" (I live three months in the spring and three months in the fall in Tavarnelle).

Before finishing my sentence, Stefania exclaimed, "What? I live in Tavarnelle!" Unbelievably, we determined that her house could be seen, looking across the vineyard out my kitchen window! What on earth are the odds?

I am beginning to understand, in my *world, the odds are pretty darn good.*

Remember the prayer I told you about at the very first of the book? Every day I pray that God would place someone in my path that could help me or that needs mine. *Every day He answers that prayer, and on this day, it was answered with my beautiful friend, Stefania.*

We made plans for dinner at my casa that week and said our goodbyes. I could not wait to get home and tell Paola, Ricca, and Frenchy about them.

It was time to leave, and with overflowing baskets, we hobbled through the walled maze of Lucca and headed home with a car full of treasures. Although my car was filled with wonderful finds, the best ones were the new friends I had made over the weekend.

THE ARTIST

Dinner in my casa with these new friends was even more special with the discovery that Stefania's adorable husband, Antonio, is an accomplished artist! Upon our meeting in Lucca, she had mentioned that he was a painter, but our conversation was brief and contained few details.

I realized I had passed Antonio's gallery in Tavarnelle every Thursday, going to the Mercato in the piazza. I admired his work in the window and wanted to see it, but the gallery was never open when I passed.

As we shared good food, great wine, and excellent stories, Frenchy serenaded us on his cello, and before the night ended, I landed an appointment at Antonio's gallery.

His gallery, yet another wonderland, was originally a hostel and stable for travelers sojourning through Tavarnelle in the early 1700s. The beautifully lit space was intimate and charming. Time-weathered terracotta bricks formed an arched ceiling, while a fabulous mosaic floor provided the perfect frame for Antonio's work. A multitude of misshapen tubes of paint resided in stacked wooden drawers, waiting for the artist's hand to invite them onto the canvas. The wooden pallet found next to his easel was yet another piece of art, merely from the vibrant colors that had been blended upon it.

Per my request, I sat and listened as Antonio described each painting. The vivid blues on each canvas were only surpassed by his deeply-set azure blue eyes. He allowed me to take photographs while he painted and as we visited. Each painting, a story. Every stroke, a feeling. Some evoked emotions of joy and triumph; others, sorrow and pain. You could feel life behind each piece and his soul through the brushstrokes upon them.

When Stefania entered the room, he lit up, and I went into full photographer mode! The two of them were dazzling together and needed to be photographed. The sun streaming in the front window played off their faces as it danced across the sea on a summer day. Watching them together and hearing their story was such a gift.

As we shared this time together, it was most evident our meeting was not a coincidence. It was divine intervention. Although each of us had carried loads that seemed too difficult to bear, we all agreed we had survived. We were stronger and had all been greatly blessed with lives we could have never imagined.

Mountains do not rise without earthquakes.

THE SURVIVORS

After a bit, Stefania left to secure a table for lunch at Caffé degli Amici, down the street. As Antonio was gathering his belongings, I noticed one painting that we had not discussed. It didn't stand out in the crowd, but it caught my eye. "Antonio, Tell me about *this* one."

"Ah, the sunflowers. This one is special. I have had it for quite some time. Oddly, several people wanted it but, for whatever reason, didn't end up taking it home. I think perhaps it was because another painting may have resonated more deeply with them. I love it and took it home. I have had it there for a few years and actually just brought it back in this morning."

The painting was a large ochre field, which clearly, at one time, had been the home of countless sunflowers. The field looked as if it had been freshly tilled, but in one corner, a small group of flowers were still standing.

"These beautiful ladies," Antonio said, "clearly at the end of their existence, were fighting to stay alive. The blade of the farmer had not yet disturbed them, and they were standing there, tall and elegant, facing the brutal sun of August. These brave ladies were the *survivors*."

As he said the word "survivor," my knees buckled, and I dropped to the small, wooden stool at my feet.

With tears swelling in my eyes, I replied, "This one is mine."

Antonio turned to me with a smile and said, "Yes, perhaps this one has been waiting for you."

My relationship with Stefania and Antonio grew as quickly and vividly as the red poppies that burst across the green fields of Val Dorcia in May and was every bit as beautiful.

I love their story. I love their work, their dogs, and their home. I love them.

Saying goodbye continues to be the most difficult thing about my time in Italy. The friends my Father continues to place along my path there have become family. Thankfully, this goodbye would be a short one as I would return in the fall with seven groups, anxious to experience *my* Tuscany.

Before leaving, it was determined that I would acquire the painting in September and that it would hang in *Casa Kima* (aka Casa Paola) until I had a place of my own. Antonio offered this beautiful piece to me at an extremely affordable price.

Did I mention he has painted for Dolce and Gabbana? Well, there is that.

Before moving to Tavarnelle, they resided in the quaint seaside village of Santa Margherita, next-door neighbor to Portofino. Private yachts occupied by the rich and famous come in and out of this port on the Italian Riviera, and his work is well-known and respected there.

His pedigree and history, however, were *not* what made me fall in love with this painting. I fell in love with the story *and* the artist...well, as much as Stefania would allow!

This *could* have been the end of the story. This story in itself is enough.

However, God, the Master Artist, still had a masterpiece that was yet to be revealed.

THE SURVIVORS

After the long journey from America, my first fall group in 2022 arrived on September 1. This group was not a typical one. I knew all of them, except one, each from my *first life*.

Oddly enough (or not), the *Hee Haw Honeys* formed one summer night after a chance meeting with my friend Kenna. We had lunch at a mutual friend's home, and I shared a chapter from the book. She had been wanting to make this trip for years and called her friend Nancy, also a dear college friend of mine, to share about our meeting.

That very night, a mutual friend of Nancy's from Alabama called her about a trip to Italy she had planned with a friend. She explained that they were looking for two others to join them, and within minutes, this group of four was created. *Again, God at work.*

What made this group rather extraordinary was that two of them had recently bonded over unspeakable losses.

One woman was grieving the loss of a beloved son, and the other, the loss of a son *and her* husband, *both within five years. Unfathomable.*

Both had *sister-friends* who had walked faithfully beside them, and I knew this would be an emotional journey for all four of them. Again, no coincidence. I knew God was working and would do some amazing things if I stayed out of His way.

I provided the platform and prayed. He created.

We shared so many mountain-top moments. Sunrise, floating quietly across the Tuscan countryside in a hot-air balloon with my friend Max, who had also recently experienced a similar loss. Breakfast with Gianna, my darling friend who is the picture of resilience, despite her circumstances. We laughed and cried as we watched the sun setting over the Ligurian sea, sitting on the turret of a Gothic castle. We twirled our pasta, ate gelato, and shopped the streets of Arezzo. We sang and danced around the Paolella family table as Frenchy played Bach and the Bee Gees.

Last but not least, we experienced art. We stood at the feet of *David* in amazement and were wowed by intricately frescoed domes within stunning cathedrals, but the most astounding art we witnessed was not from the hands of those talented Renaissance artists.

THE MASTERPIECE

After sharing my story of Stefania and Antonio, Stacey expressed wanting to find an artist who could paint the last picture she had taken of her son. The other ladies also expressed wanting to obtain a special piece of art, so I contacted Stefania right away. That afternoon, we were invited to their beautiful home. Introductions were made, and *the rest of the story* began.

I remember quietly reclining on their faded chintz sofas and seeing it all unfold. I watched as each woman *pulled out* the blank, painful canvases of their stories and carefully presented them to Antonio. I witnessed these *survivors* allow themselves to be vulnerable, to open the wounds of their hearts, and allow tiny bits of healing to occur. Antonio handled each one so tenderly and respectfully. It was a most sacred time.

The paintings commissioned that afternoon now reside in the homes of my friends. Each piece serves as a reminder of this special trip; the memories and friends made there. Most of all, these paintings serve as a reminder of their subjects and the people who love them.

Although I was privileged to witness this incredible moment in Italy...I realize the bigger masterpiece is the one that the Father created for *all* of us.

The *moment* He created before going to Italy was ever even a passing thought for them or *for me*. Before the pain. Before the loss.

Have you ever watched an artist do a painting in real time? This was what I witnessed.

Oh, by the way, guess what Nancy asked Antonio to paint for her.

A field of sunflowers that her husband Ty secretly planted for her... *before his passing.*

Grazie Dio. Thank you for the earthquakes and *the mountains.*

RMS TITANIC, ON APRIL 19, 1912 JUST PRIOR TO SETTING SAIL FROM
SOUTHAMPTON'S WHITE STAR DOCK ON HER MAIDEN VOYAGE TO NEW YORK.

CHAPTER 19

The Unsinkable Titanic

Pride leads to disgrace, but with humility comes wisdom.

—PROVERBS 11:2 (NLT)

In one of my favorite movies, *Steel Magnolias*, Truvy Jones says, "Laughter through tears is one of my favorite emotions." I couldn't agree with her more, and I think every story needs a good dose of both!

Why is it that so many funny stories occur surrounding weddings?

It was the summer of 1981, and twin sisters from a very prominent Nashville family were having a double wedding. It was to be *the* wedding of the season! Fortunately, I was friends with one of the girls and checked our mailbox every day, anxiously awaiting the invitation.

In my humble opinion, attending a good Southern church wedding is better than a trip to Disney World, and this one was going to be a doozie! I frantically began the search for a perfect ensemble to wear to this exciting event.

I was in the best shape of my life at the time, as I spent around six to eight hours a day on the tennis court. I was fit as a fiddle, in my prime, *and ready for my close-up* at this event. Although I cannot find a picture, I do remember buying a fetching red dress and shiny red patent leather pumps. I also distinctly remember feeling *really* good about myself. *Actually, too good.* Hmmm...I believe there's a scripture out there about that.

Always the last one to run out the door, I flitted down the stairs and jumped into the car while still putting on my *finishing touches.*

When we arrived, I emerged from our Chevrolet Impala like Elizabeth Taylor arriving on the red carpet. But where were my paparazzi?

As I entered the vestibule of the church, I immediately felt all eyes turn on me and basked in the attention. To my delight, I was even escorted by one of the most eligible BMOCs (big men on campus), on whom I had an enormous crush.

Clinging to his arm, I sashayed all the way down the aisle to the fourth row and, with a nod, gestured thank you to my handsome escort *as if we had been on a date.* I lowered myself as gracefully as possible, given my three-inch stiletto pumps.

My parents and sister sat to my left, and on my right was university Spanish professor Gladys Gooch. *Yes, this was her real name*, which makes this story even better!

As the prelude began, Professor Gooch and I struck up a conversation. While we were whispering about *global peace*, I felt a slight tremor on the pew. I turned to my left and found all three of my family members bent over, snickering. I was deeply involved in *lofty* conversations with Señorita Gooch and rolled my eyes, apologizing for their unruly behavior.

As the strings began to play "Send in the Clowns" *(no joke)*, the pew began to quake even harder. I turned again to my family and noticed that tears were now streaming down my sister's face. In disdain, I asked what in the world was so funny. She was unable to even utter a word. Now I was downright embarrassed and pressed her for an answer!

Literally heaving and doubled over, she reached up to grasp *her* hair and gesture to *mine*. She did it several times. By this point, my father's laughter had progressed into a low wheeze, and my mother had buried her face in her hands. Finally, my sister regained composure just long enough to eke out, "Kim...your...your...your hair."

In that moment, it hit me.

Full of dread, I reached up to the left side of my head (yes, the escorted side) and discovered an enormous pink sponge roller; this specimen being the *biggest jumbo size* ever known to mankind that, in my harried state, had accidentally been *left in my perfectly coiffed hair*. I literally melted into the pew and ripped this *uninvited guest* from its reserved seat.

Needless to say, *I walked out a little differently than when I walked in.*

PRIDE GOES BEFORE THE FALL

Years later, when teaching the senior high girls' class at our home congregation, this was the perfect illustration of *pride going before the fall.* I always finished the class with a reminder to the girls. *Just when you think you are all that and have arrived, check your hair for a pink sponge roller or your shoe for a toilet paper trail!*

I share this story for two reasons.

First, it's a great story, *and Boy Wonder insisted.* I needed to be taken down a notch or two, and this definitely did the job. I have never used a pink sponge roller since. The sight of one evokes severe trauma *and* nausea!

All laughter aside, I share this story because it was a very valuable lesson learned early in life. How I wish I could say this lesson did the trick forever, *but it did not.*

I have never considered myself to be prideful. I have striven to purposefully give God the glory for every gift which He has so abundantly given.

However, I may have discovered another form of pride that I might have missed.

Maybe sometimes *basking in these gifts* can cloud our vision and prevent us from seeing imminent danger signs along the way. I realize now these signs are also valuable *gifts* from the Father.

Perhaps while riding upon the waves of grand experiences, I missed the hurricane into which I was headed. *I missed every red flag.*

I am *not* saying it is wrong to rejoice in the blessings and successes of life. The Father has given them and loves bringing joy to His children. I am merely suggesting to be mindful and aware, especially during the glorious times of life. Watch for warning signs. *Red flags are designed for a reason.* I pay much closer attention to them now.

THE RMS TITANIC

On April 15, 1912, the RMS *Titanic* sank to its watery grave at the bottom of the Atlantic Ocean. Just four days before, more than two thousand passengers and crew members boarded the vessel—the largest and most luxurious passenger ship of its time.

Each passenger and crew member was confident that the *Titanic* would safely transport them from Southampton, England, to their final destination, New York City, in only eight days.

The *Titanic* tragedy claimed the lives of more than 1,500 people. Although this disaster took the ship—and the entire world—by surprise, it didn't come without warning. The *Titanic* officers *received multiple ice warnings* yet didn't bother to slow down or change their course.

The officers were caught up in the excitement of the voyage and *distracted* with their various duties and social engagements. *They didn't take the warning signs seriously.* They reasoned that if an iceberg was present, they would see it in plenty of time to change their course and avoid collision.

Thomas Andrews, chief designer and naval architect of the *RMS Titanic,* was in his cabin, planning *cosmetic changes* he wanted to make on the ship as the ship struck the iceberg. *He also perished in the disaster.*

In the Oscar-winning movie *Titanic,* reveling is depicted

on board as Bruce Ismay, the highest-ranking White Star official; Andrews, its architect; and others celebrated last moments on the *unsinkable Titanic*...all the while, an iceberg of unfathomable size lurked beneath the icy waters of the Atlantic only miles ahead.

Would the story have ended differently had they paid attention? More attention to details and warnings; less resting on the laurels of their success?

Perhaps they should have checked for the pink sponge roller.

THE SEMMERING PASS

CHAPTER 20

Climb Every Mountain

The best thing is yet to be.

—ROBERT BROWNING

Upon my first visit to Monteriggioni, I carefully eased down the herringbone path, stepping into the light that streamed through Porta di Ponente. My travel partner had hiked on down the hill, and I stood there alone.

Like a Greek siren, the sun's brilliant rays beckoned me closer to the opening of this ancient fortress. This mystical view held me captive in a trance. The wind blowing through the arch felt as if the very breath of God was caressing my face, and as I gazed up into the heavens, I knew this was an epiphany that would change my life forever.

Wanting to remember this moment, I steadied my iPhone and snapped the picture that occupies the front and back covers of this book. This arch, one which I dare say has been the frame for many a romantic kiss or embrace, was the gateway for the new life that awaited me on the other side. Unbelievably, this site, which is usually brimming with camera-clad tourists, on *this day* was abandoned.

It was May, and the panoramic canvas before me was painted in every single shade of green, then glazed with a golden umber, which was the sun setting behind the foothills of Siena. A dotting of terracotta roofs could hardly be seen due to the burgeoning foliage now growing over each house. It was obvious the earth was slowly awakening from the cold days of winter and in a state of rebirth. *So was I.*

Although I knew this was *a moment*, I had no comprehension of the events that would follow.

I may have missed a few *road signs* along the way of life (okay, some, major billboards!), but it didn't take a rocket scientist to figure out I was being sent a *new roadmap* and direction.

Within a few months and after a great deal of planning, I was sitting behind the wheel in Italy, making plans for my first season of guests *and a new season of life.* The thought of even going to Italy was beyond my wildest comprehension, and yet here I was. I felt much like Maria singing "I Have Confidence" as I was rounding every corner in my little rented Fiat!

THE NEXT KILIMANJARO

Several years after my arrival in Italy, I was talking to a dear friend who was instrumental in facilitating that new season.

Actually, the aforementioned *epiphany* occurred during my first opportunity of working with him and his wife on a two-year residential contract in Guntersville, Alabama. Thankfully, this job afforded me time and means to return and make necessary plans for the new business venture in Italy.

Steve is a bit of an adventure-seeker himself. After seeing photographs of all their world travels, I transferred over one hundred of them to canvases and displayed them on the walls of their media room. One of my favorites was a series of photos of Steve in Antarctica doing the polar bear plunge into twenty-eight-degree water!

However, there was one photo *and excursion* missing from his bucket list. Summiting Mount Kilimanjaro.

Over nine months of planning and training were spent with three of his best buddies...all *Indiana Jones look-alikes.* On a cold January morning in 2022, the Facebook post was made. They all successfully reached the summit! *This* treasured canvas now has an honored place on those walls.

After Steve's return from the summit, we had an interesting discussion that resonated very deeply with me.

A well-meaning church friend commented to him, "Well, Steve, I don't guess you can ever top that one!"

I explained that several people had made similar comments to me about my moment in the arch. While *both* moments were clearly once-in-a-lifetime events, we each had similar feelings about those comments.

At Steve's age, there will probably never be another summit that will surpass Kilimanjaro. It stretched his body and its abilities to the limit and then some.

At mine, it is doubtful I will have another encounter quite like the epiphanic one standing in the sunset-bathed arch of Monteriggioni. It was life-transforming.

Although these events have made lasting impressions on our lives, we both agreed that we will *never* stop looking for the next *wonder* and will continue the climb. *There will still be more Kilimanjaros and Monteriggionis.*

The next *wonder* might be an unexpected one and arrive in a humbler setting.

THE BOOK REVIEW

Recently, I received a text from a woman who had been *placed in my path* during the darkest days of the pandemic. The week before this conversation, she made a positive comment on a post concerning progress on the book. My editor had advised sharing my work with friends and family to solicit objective criticism. I knew she was a retired educator, librarian, and an avid reader; therefore, she was a perfect candidate. She was thrilled with the opportunity of reading my work and heartily accepted the invitation.

When she called, she asked if I had time to listen as she needed my full attention. I was driving and pulled into the closest parking lot and anxiously waited to hear her review. Instead, she began with a very different story that began in the spring of 2020.

She shared that the past seven years had been extremely difficult. She had been forced into early retirement from a job she loved, working with underserved children in the Metro Nashville school system. This while dealing with challenging health issues of her own *and* losing her mother. Her words were *devastating*. Mounted upon these trials was dealing with a global pandemic. She continued by confiding in me that during this period, she had even contemplated ending her life.

Thankfully, a mutual friend of ours recognized her signs of depression and suggested that she might enjoy watching my cooking classes on *Facebook Live*. At that time, someone asked me to demonstrate making sourdough bread, and before I knew it, I was doing online classes two to three times a week.

She tuned in for my very first class and said that although she did not know me from Adam's housecat, my little *show* made her feel like she had a new friend, *as I had called her by name*. It made her laugh and was a bright spot in her day. What she didn't know was that those classes actually kept me connected and sane during that horribly isolating time in *my* life.

As the months passed, hers was *always* the first name to pop up and comment, each time leaving positive remarks. She also supported me by ordering several cookbooks and to-go meals, which had become *my* means of support during the shutdown.

One day I received a precious hand-written note and gift for my new grandbaby, who was getting a good bit of air-time with Nonna's bragging!

While listening to her go *on and on* about how *I had helped her* through that crazy time, I reflected on the encouragement *she had been to me*.

Within minutes, she moved into notes that she had made about each chapter.

She understood every metaphor. She explained eloquently how each story resonated with her. One passage in particular that she loved was the explanation of how helping others actually helped me. She explained this advice of putting this act into practice had moved *her* to a better place.

She finished by thanking me for sharing hope and joy, even while I was experiencing difficulties of my own.

Let me be perfectly clear; *there will* never *be a book review written that will* ever *mean more to me than this one. Nothing will equal her words.* She *is the very reason why this book was written. If she is the only person in the entire world who gets it, my writing has served a purpose.*

This *was my next Kilimanjaro.* Another summit, but this one, in the front seat of my Honda Pilot.

No pictures were made or memorabilia saved. Only the beautiful treasure of her words, which now proudly reside upon the walls of my heart.

LESSONS TO BE LEARNED

First of all, after your big moments, *keep climbing* and expecting wonderful outcomes. Also, continue climbing despite failures and disappointment.

One of my all-time favorite quotes is from Olympic skater Scott Hamilton. "I've calculated that over the course of my skating career, I fell over 41,600 times. And you know what? I got back up 41,600 times! Get up!"

Get up! Life will *not* pick you up. Get up and keep climbing and looking for the magical moments.

Do not, however, only look for magic in the *big* days.

Sometimes—many times—His best work is done quietly. These small moments can also be *summits*.

Secondly, never underestimate the power your words or actions may have in the life of someone.

Simple words and actions can create someone else's Kilimanjaro. They can be *their* next big moment. Do not ever think that you are too small, insignificant, or too old to make a huge impact in the lives of others.

Be kind. Kind words can entirely change the trajectory of someone else's life.

During *my storm*, many times, people would turn and walk the other way. I honestly do not believe there was malice or ill will in their actions. I cannot even tell you how many times I have heard the statement "I just didn't know what to say."

Allow me to be blunt. *Say* something. *Please say something.*

Saying "I love you...I am praying for you...I am thinking about you" is *never the wrong thing to say. Ever.*

The person you are afraid to say *the wrong thing* to may possibly be dangling by a thread ready to break. You might be saying the *only* words that keep them from putting a gun to their head.

SAYING GOODBYE

Writing this book has been quite a journey.

I am *not* a good editor. I have struggled with too many words in every chapter, going back over and over, deleting, changing, and reworking everything before handing it over.

This final chapter has truly been my nemesis. Writing it feels like preparing to say goodbye to a very dear friend for the last time. You want your final words to be meaningful and impactful. You pray every reader walks away feeling encouraged, inspired, and loved. For each and every reader has given me the greatest gift of all...their time, which is fleeting.

For obvious reasons, one of my favorite books and movies is Frances Mayes' *Under the Tuscan Sun*. One of the most poignant moments is when Frances, who is completely despondent, has a meltdown over the loss of her marriage *and* the fact that *she has bought a house in Italy for a life she doesn't even have.*

After an encounter with an unwanted guest in her ancient house, she frantically calls her friend and handsome realtor for help. As he pokes around in the fireplace, he relays this story, "Signora, between Austria and Italy, there is a section of the Alps called the Semmering. It is an impossibly steep, very high part of the mountains. They built a train track over these Alps to connect Vienna and Venice. They built these tracks even before there was a train in existence that could make the trip. They built it because they knew someday, the train would come."

At the end of the story, Frances recalls the above and makes this statement, "Any arbitrary turn along the way, and I would be elsewhere. I would be different. Unthinkably good things can happen, even late in the game. It is such a surprise."

Boy, can I relate to her feelings.

It is so easy to fall into the trap of feeling *finished*—especially following a mountain-top experience. It may, however, be even more tempting to *be done* after a traumatic or difficult occurrence in your life. Death, divorce, illness, empty nest...the list is endless.

I am living proof that there is so *much more out there if you believe that good things will still come and continue to climb. Life can be such a surprise!*

Now, I will absolutely guarantee that you will get many cuts and bruises along the way. But, I promise, the journey will be so worth the risk.

As I was trying to leave you with an inspirational quote, like a good Singarama director, my mind automatically turned to music. For over thirty years, I have heard songs on the radio and thought, *Oh, that would be a perfect Singarama finale!* I guess I am now searching for that great finale, but this time no song or dance; this one, to be read.

One song that immediately came to my mind is more familiar to me than all the *Partridge Family* tunes, which still spin on the turntable of my mind!

This song is taken from *my* first favorite movie, which, depending on your age, and gender, is probably at the top of *your* list as well.

If asked to do so, I could recite every word in the script *and* sing every verse of every single song, backward *and* standing on my head. I can also greatly identify with the lead character, who was a bit of a *whirling dervish* herself.

When Maria was at the crossroads of her life, she was sent

to the Mother Abbess, who sang those legendary lyrics over her. Although I have sung them all my life, one line jumped out that I had never really noticed. The Reverend Mother beautifully encouraged Maria to keep climbing and searching each and every day of her life for as long as she lived. Not only when she was happy or fulfilled.

I will close by asking, are you still climbing? Are you still laying rails upon your track?

The decision is completely up to you.

However, do not wait on new adventures without climbing or expect a train to arrive if you are not willing to step out in faith that it will.

There are always new rails to be placed, new mountains to climb, puzzles to begin.

I believe the Master Artist is using ALL my broken pieces to complete His masterpiece in me.

He can do the same for you.

ABOUT THE AUTHOR

Kimberly Stansbury Whitaker is a child of Nashville who divides her days between the warmth of her cottage in Tennessee and the wonder of a farm in the heart of Tuscany, where many of these stories have occurred.

Her busy life as a mother (now *nonna*), interior designer, chef and cookbook writer, event and travel planner, and successful bag designer placed her on *Oprah's Favorite Things list*, *The Today Show*, and *QVC*. Her extraordinary life has been filled with the *highest highs and lowest lows*.

Kim's surrender to the One who created all the pieces has helped her realize the purpose of every one of them in her life and ultimately led her to write *Finding the Pieces*.

Connect with Kim on Facebook and Instagram or at *www.flourishstyle.net*, *or perhaps even cross paths with her at the Storico Mercato Centrale in Firenze if you happen by in the spring or fall.*

Printed in the USA
CPSIA information can be obtained
at www.ICGtesting.com
LVHW011358111223
766208LV00001B/1

9 798890 41456